CW00515729

Content

The John Clare Society Journal

The official Journal of the John Clare Society,
published annually to reflect the interest in, and approaches to,
the life and work of the poet John Clare.

Editor
Simon Kövesi
(Oxford Brookes University)

Reviews Editor
Erin Lafford (University of Oxford)

Advisory Board
Jonathan Bate (Arizona State University)
Gerard Carruthers (University of Glasgow)
Katey Castellano (James Madison University)
Paul Chirico (Fitzwilliam College, Cambridge)
Johanne Clare (George Brown College, Toronto)
Richard Cronin (University of Glasgow)
Paul Farley (Lancaster University)
John Gardner (Anglia Ruskin University)
John Goodridge (Nottingham Trent University)
Nick Groom (University of Macau)
Robert Heyes (John Clare Society)
Andrew Hodgson (University of Birmingham)
C. M. Jackson-Houlston (Oxford Brookes University)
Bridget Keegan (Creighton University, Omaha)
Peter Kitson (University of East Anglia)
Donna Landry (University of Kent)
Emma Mason (University of Warwick)
Scott McEathron (Southern Illinois University)
Jerome McGann (University of Virginia)
James McKusick (University of Missouri–Kansas City)
Nicholas Roe (University of St Andrews)
Adam Rounce (University of Nottingham)
Simon Sanada (Aichi University, Japan)
Fiona Stafford (Somerville College, Oxford)
Sarah Zimmerman (Fordham University)

Number 40 July 2021

The John Clare Society

The John Clare Society is a UK Registered Charity, number 1124846

New members are always welcome; please contact Dr Robert Heyes,
53 Judd Road, Tonbridge, Kent, TN9 2NH
Email: bob.heyes@yahoo.co.uk

For journal submission details, please email or write to the Editor:
skovesi@brookes.ac.uk, Professor Simon Kövesi,
English and Modern Languages, Oxford Brookes University, OX3 0BP, UK

AFFILIATED
SOCIETY

© 2021 published by the John Clare Society
Printed by: Joshua Horgan, 246 Marston Road, Oxford OX3 0E
www.joshuahorgan.co.uk

ISBN 978-1-9161355-3-6

This is a limited edition of 500, free to full members of the Society,

£7.00 if purchased separately.

Editorial

This issue marks another significant anniversary in the John Clare calendar: the bicentenary of the publication of his second collection, *The Village Minstrel and Other Poems.* As we did for issue 39, this year we commissioned scholars to write five-hundred-word studies of their favourite poems from the 1821 collection. In one instance we are able to present in public for the first time what might be the earliest set of written responses to Clare's book, in the shape of annotations by the poet's devoted friend and ally Eliza Emmerson. We are grateful to the anonymous owner for allowing access to these rare treasures. Also in the same manner as last year, we have allowed this journal to be much larger than usual, in an effort to go some way to compensate society members for another summer without a festival, or any *Village Minstrel* anniversary events for that matter.

The front cover image is of Mihály Munkácsy's 'Woman Carrying Brushwood' (1873), reproduced by kind permission of the SzépművészetiMúzeum, Museum of Fine Arts, Budapest, Hungary, © 2021. The editor would like to thank art historian Dr Nóra Veszprémi of the University of Birmingham for alerting him to this work. Dr Veszprémi tweets about Hungarian nineteenth-century art @NVeszpremi.

Simon Kövesi
Oxford Brookes University

Detail from 'Going Home', Fritz von Uhde (German, 1848–1911),
c. 1889, oil on wood. The Metropolitan Museum of Art, New York.

Anniversary Shorts:

Studies of *The Village Minstrel, and Other Poems*
London: Taylor and Hessey, 1821

September 1821 saw Clare's second collection of verse published, in two volumes. The short essays below form a celebration of this major publication, which saw Clare flex his literary muscles in forms and modes far beyond the reach of *Poems Descriptive* of 1820. Nine of the essays are focused on particular poems from this book – and texts (or extracts of longer poems) are printed just before each of the studies, as they were presented in print in 1821, and in order of their original appearance. The tenth piece, by Sir Jonathan Bate, is a transcription of what must be the first written response to the publication, by Clare's most ardent of correspondents, Eliza Emmerson. – Simon Kövesi

THE

VILLAGE MINSTREL,

AND

OTHER POEMS.

BY JOHN CLARE,

THE NORTHAMPTONSHIRE PEASANT;

AUTHOR OF "POEMS ON RURAL LIFE AND SCENERY."

" I never list presume to Parnasse Hill,
" But piping low, in shade of lowly grove,
" I play to please myself."------
Spenser's Shep. Kal.

AFTER READING IN A LETTER

PROPOSALS FOR BUILDING A COTTAGE.

Beside a runnel build my shed,
  With stubbles cover'd o'er;
Let broad oaks o'er its chimney spread,
  And grass-plats grace the door.

The door may open with a string,
  So that it closes tight;
And locks would be a wanted thing,
  To keep out thieves at night.

A little garden, not too fine,
  Inclose with painted pales;
And woodbines, round the cot to twine,
  Pin to the wall with nails.

Let hazels grow, and spindling sedge,
  Bent bowering over-head;
Dig old man's beard from woodland hedge,
  To twine a summer shade.

Beside the threshold sods provide,
  And build a summer seat;
Plant sweet-briar bushes by its side,
  And flowers that blossom sweet.

I love the sparrow's ways to watch
  Upon the cotter's sheds,
So here and there pull out the thatch,
  That they may hide their heads.

And as the sweeping swallows stop
  Their flights along the green,
Leave holes within the chimney-top
  To paste their nest between.

Stick shelves and cupboards round the hut,
  In all the holes and nooks;
Nor in the corner fail to put
  A cupboard for the books.

Along the floor some sand I'll sift,
  To make it fit to live in;
And then I'll thank ye for the gift,
  As something worth the giving.

John Goodridge

I am often drawn to this little poem (see my *John Clare and Community*), because although it is a familiar genre piece (the 'wish' poem, influenced by John Pomfret's popular poem 'The Choice'), Clare makes it his own, and it reflects his sense of where and how he would like to live, had he world enough and time. We do not know what the 'letter' of the title was that stimulated him to write, but certainly the question of what to 'do' with Clare once he had been 'discovered' and published—how to groom and maintain and house him—much preoccupied his various patrons through the 1820s and 1830s in their paternalistic way, a process that led in 1832 to finding him a cottage to rent in the fenland village of Northborough, four miles and a world away, hoping he would set up as a smallholder ('Farmer John', as Eliza Emmerson well-meaningly dubbed him). When his mental health deteriorated badly five years later, they arranged for him to be sent away to an outwardly respectable private asylum in Epping Forest.

Where would Clare really like to have lived? His 'dream home' is clearly laid out in these simple lines, and it is a most interesting one. It would be 'beside a runnel', a small stream that will give him water and natural music. His home is described in a way that is literally and entirely designed to blend in with nature, not through visual trickery of any kind, but by being made of natural products (oak, hazel, straw thatch, grass, woodbine, sand: we can overlook his 'nails', 'string' and 'locks'), and designed to be protected, colonised, even absorbed by nature. Broad oaks protect it, growing grass plats cover and decorate the entrance, hazel boughs embower the place, and the thatch is to be pulled out 'here and there' for the birds to inhabit, regardless of the consequent considerable risk of rain leakage. The floor is simply loose sand, the garden wild enough to qualify as 'not too fine', and the only interior objects here are (wooden) shelves and cupboards, especially a corner cupboard 'for the books': an artificial leisure product, but arguably one made largely from natural materials. Clare also manufactured his own ink from oak-galls, recycled tea and sugar wrappers for writing paper, even used a dusty barn wall for geometrical drawings. Despite Robert Heyes calling him out as an ecological vandal for his egg and plant collecting (present again here), Clare was instinctively an ecological thinker in the broader sense. He wants his ideal house engulfed by nature, made with natural products, to live peacefully within her bounds in a thoroughly Thoreauesque way.

Could Clare possibly be laughing, finally, at those well-meaning patrons, with their sensible schemes and practical plans for him, chivvying him to marry his pregnant girlfriend, thinking about income and interest, family life and sobriety? Yet it seems all the poet really wanted was a safe haven in the woods, lost in nature.

'Cooling the Porridge', Jean-François Millet (French, 1814–1875), 1861, etching on laid paper. The Metropolitan Museum of Art, New York.

TO AN INFANT DAUGHTER.

Sweet gem of infant fairy-flowers!
Thy smiles on life's unclosing hours,
Like sunbeams lost in summer showers,
    They wake my fears;
When reason knows its sweets and sours,
    They'll change to tears.

God help thee, little senseless thing!
Thou, daisy-like of early spring,
Of ambush'd winter's hornet sting
    Hast yet to tell;
Thou know'st not what to-morrows bring:
    I wish thee well.

But thou art come, and soon or late
'Tis thine to meet the frowns of fate,
The harpy grin of envy's hate,
    And mermaid-smiles
Of worldly folly's luring bait,
    That youth beguiles.

And much I wish, whate'er may be
The lot, my child, that falls to thee,
Nature may never let thee see
    Her glass betimes,
But keep thee from my failings free,—
    Nor itch at rhymes.

Lord knows my heart, it loves thee much;
And may my feelings, aches, and such,
The pains I meet in folly's clutch
    Be never thine:
Child, it's a tender string to touch,
    That sounds "thou'rt mine."

Valerie Pedlar

The poem opens with Clare's tender apostrophe to his new daughter expressing his appreciation of the beauty, the preciousness, yet the fragility of the baby (Anna Maria was born 2 June 1820). A gem is substantial enough, but the idea of 'fairy-flowers' – lovely though it is – suggests the ephemeral, a suggestion that is echoed in the simile that follows comparing the baby's smiles to 'sunbeams lost in summer showers'. By the end of the stanza, however, smiles have turned to tears, and what might have been an ode to a new baby, becomes a grimmer poem, the father's delight displaced by fears.

The natural imagery associated with the baby disappears as the poet imagines the 'frowns of fate' that surely await the child. His fears for her future are apparently predicated on his own experience: achieving success and thus arousing envy and hatred on the one hand, or on the other hand falling prey to the follies of youth. There is no suggestion of a happy future, or indeed of ways in which he might help her through life. The imagery in this third stanza, combining abstract nouns, human facial expressions and the fantastical ('harpy grin', 'mermaid-smiles') gives the verse great intensity and indicates a speaker who is out of joint with society. Furthermore, as the poem progresses we get the impression of a man who is not at ease with himself.

In the fourth stanza Clare voices a puzzling wish: that Nature should 'never let thee see / Her glass betimes'. This could mean that he hopes the difficulties of life do not displace the carefree life of childhood too soon. But because the next line, separated only by a comma, expresses the hope that she will escape his 'failings', it might imply that he hopes his daughter will never see in *him* failings or a fate that might be hers too; his articulated wish is that she might be free of these failings. In particular he wishes that she may never experience his 'itch at rhymes', an expression that conveys the discomfort as well as the compulsion of his need to write. However, it is not only his 'failings' but his 'feelings', and the 'clutch' of 'folly' that he hopes she will avoid. 'Folly', which in stanza three apparently means 'foolishness', must be interpreted in the final stanza as 'mental derangement'. This meaning is confirmed in one of the two stanzas in the manuscript version of this poem that are omitted in the 1821 publication: 'L—d help thee in thy coming years / If thy mad fathers picture 'pears / Predominant' (*Early Poems*, II, p. 392, ll. 25-7).

Clare expresses his deep love for the child, but whereas the good fairies may bring wishes of health and happiness, he can only wish that his daughter may be free of the disadvantages threatening her both by inheritance and through circumstance. His final words, 'thou'rt mine', express a loving acknowledgement of paternity, but at the same time imply a fear of what that paternity might entail.

LANGLEY BUSH.

O Langley Bush! the shepherd's sacred shade,
    Thy hollow trunk oft gain'd a look from me;
Full many a journey o'er the heath I've made,
    For such-like curious things I love to see.
What truth the story of the swain allows,
    That tells of honours which thy young days knew,
Of "Langley Court" being kept beneath thy boughs
    I cannot tell—thus much I know is true,
That thou art reverenc'd: even the rude clan
    Of lawless gipsies, driven from stage to stage,
Pilfering the hedges of the husbandman,
    Spare thee, as sacred, in thy withering age,
Both swains and gipsies seem to love thy name,
    Thy spot's a favourite with the sooty crew,
And soon thou must depend on gipsy-fame,
    Thy mouldering trunk is nearly rotten through.
My last doubts murmur on the zephyr's swell,
    My last look lingers on thy boughs with pain;
To thy declining age I bid farewel,
    Like old companions, ne'er to meet again.

Emma Mason

The opening clause of this poem—'O Langley Bush!'—calls to a
dying and ancient hawthorn who has long sheltered shepherds,
swains, gipsies, and poets. First recorded in a grant of land from
948, the tree was known to locals as a Bronze age barrow, a Roman
shrine, an intersection of four parishes—Helpston, Ailsworth,
Ufford, and Upton—and the shadowy site of a gibbet. Clare recalls
this in his reference to 'Langley Court', an Anglo-Saxon chancery
where criminals were tried twice yearly by the Langdyke Hundred.
Here is a tree who shielded sinners and lawbreakers under its
'reverenc'd' branches and boughs until the hangman interceded.
These 'honours' of its 'young days' invite the reader into stories
and ritual meanings in which Clare rejoiced: 'For such-like curious
things I love to see'. Langley Bush both symbolizes and incarnates
the mutuality of nature, the divine, and the human, and offers
acceptance and refuge to those without safe haven: Clare on his
journeys 'o'er the heath', shepherds in need of a well-earned nap,

and gipsies dependent on its wood for warmth. Reversing Harry Gill's treatment of Goody Blake in Wordsworth's lyrical ballad, Clare's tree freely offers itself for 'pilfering', and it is praised by all who find solace there as a 'favourite' 'spot' for quietude, prayer, and communal talk.

A 'sacred shade', the Langley Bush of *The Village Minstrel* is uncomfortable with the manuscript's 'smutty crew' who seek solace in its dwelling space. This version prefers 'sooty crew', a racialised description that reveals the gipsies' social and cultural displacement as well as their dependence on this treescape commons. It also reminds us how closely they sit by a fire kindled by the tree's offerings, its body now 'hollow', and its 'mouldering trunk' 'nearly rotten through'. While a smutty, lewd bunch might not be thought up to the task of remembering and narrating the name and spirit of the dying tree, Clare embraces the 'lawless gipsies' as exactly those who will best reverence their tree companion. Any 'doubts' Clare has that its sacred being will not be memorialised or sustained are taken, he writes, by the 'zephyr's swell' and his goodbyes are given in a state of lingering and sorrowful pain. And yet in death the tree is of the living: the manuscript's preference for 'mulldering' to describe the trunk recalls the word 'muld'—a tribute or offering—so gesturing to Langley Bush as a sacrifice, perhaps a crucifixion, for those dependent on its spiritual meaning as much as its material sanctuary. Its destruction is less about enclosure (Clare's much-quoted journal entry in which he records the destruction of Langley Bush is dated 29 September 1824; the poem is written between 1818 and 1820) than remembering the sacred as integral not supplemental to existence. By 1832, Clare will lament in his poem 'Remembrances' that the 'eternal' 'raptures' the tree once promised are now fenced off; 'Langley Bush' reminds us of their perpetuity in the stories and songs of the lost and lawless.

THE LAST OF MARCH.

WRITTEN AT LOLHAM BRIGS

[Stanzas 8–9 and 11–14]

Yon bullocks low their liberty,
  The young grass cropping to their fill;
And colts, from straw-yards neighing free,
  Spring's opening promise 'joy at will:
  Along the bank, beside the rill
The happy lambkins bleat and run,
  Then weary, 'neath a sheltering hill
Drop basking in the gleaming sun.

At distance from the water's edge,
  On hanging sallow's farthest stretch,
The moor-hen 'gins her nest of sedge
  Safe from destroying school-boy's reach.
  Fen sparrows chirp and fly to fetch
The wither'd reed-down rustling nigh,
  And, by the sunny side the ditch,
Prepare their dwelling warm and dry. [...]

Ere yet a hailstone pattering comes,
  Or dimps the pool the rainy squall,
One hears, in mighty murmuring hums,
  The spirit of the tempest call:
  Here sheltering 'neath the ancient wall
I still pursue my musing dreams,
  And as the hailstones round me fall
I mark their bubbles in the streams.

Reflection here is warm'd to sigh,
  Tradition gives these brigs renown,
Though heedless Time long pass'd them by
  Nor thought them worthy noting down:
  Here in the mouth of every clown
The "Roman road" familiar sounds;
  All else, with everlasting frown,
Oblivion's mantling mist surrounds.

These walls the work of Roman hands!
  How may conjecturing Fancy pore,

As lonely here one calmly stands,
    On paths that age has trampled o'er.
    The builders' names are known no more;
No spot on earth their memory bears;
    And crowds, reflecting thus before,
Have since found graves as dark as theirs.

The storm has ceas'd,—again the sun
    The ague-shivering season dries;
Short-winded March, thou'lt soon be done,
    Thy fainting tempest mildly dies.
    Soon April's flowers and dappled skies
Shall spread a couch for lovely May,
    Upon whose bosom Nature lies
And smiles her joyous youth away.

Scott McEathron

The 'Lolham Brigs' (or bridges) of this marvellous poem's subtitle
– a series of stone spans over a south branch of the River Welland
– sit just over a mile northwest of Helpston. The topography
is precisely described by E. Barbara Dean in the second-ever
instalment of this journal (1983), in which she speculates that an
1811 signature carved into one of the bridges might well be Clare's,
and the location appears several times in his poems and journals.
Lolham Brigs was one of the more striking landmarks within
Clare's orbit, though in some seasons of the year it was a strikingly
dreary one. This is certainly the impression that John Taylor had
when he toured the spot with Clare a few months after the poem's
composition, calling it 'nothing but a dull line of ponds, or rather
one continuous marsh'.

There was nothing dreary about the spot on the March day that
inspired the poem. Over a series of fourteen stanzas in the eight-
line ballade form Clare expounds giddily on the evidence that
spring is coming fast. In some ways it is the sheer length of his
catalogue that is most noticeable, for Clare keeps enumerating the
signs of spring long past the moment when he had made his point.
Having described the 'antique elder bud[ding] anew', the 'bulrush
sprouting tall', and the 'Larks ris[ing] to meet hail the peeping sun',
still he goes on: there are robins, rooks, and 'startling peewits', the
moor-hen building a 'nest of sedge' and fen-sparrows 'by the sunny

side of the ditch / prepar[ing] their dwelling warm and dry'. One is reminded of Wordsworth's 'Written in March', but if Wordsworth's poem achieves a simple, undiluted exuberance, it nonetheless looks a little thin alongside Clare's.

Over its final four stanzas, the poem takes a brief turn: the sudden arrival of hail, wind, and rain drives the poet to shelter under the 'ancient wall' of one of the bridges. Clare withdraws from the immediacy of nature, contemplating first the stonework around him and then, in a rapidly-developing enlargement of his frame, the long human history of this locale. Cycling through a flurry of emotions and observations, he both feels the pleasurable play of his 'Fancy' in contemplating the structure's original Roman builders and laments the anonymity into which all mortals pass.

Clare may have been wrong in believing that the bridge's walls were 'the work of Roman hands' – the spans themselves were constructed in the seventeenth and eighteenth centuries – but the road that crossed them was indeed Roman, today called King Street. 'Here in the mouths of every clown', he writes, 'The "Roman road" familiar sounds'. This querulous sentiment may initially seem as obscure as the 'mantling mist' that still surrounds him, but, as in Thomas Hardy's brief lyric 'The Roman Road', it contemplates the domestication of venerable antiquity at the hands of the locals. For Hardy, this domestication was never a problem – the phrase and the place were inextricable from his memory of his mother – and Clare's own irritation here is short-lived. The storm ceases and the sun comes back out, making way for 'April's flowers and dappled skies'.

'A View of Fair Mead Bottom Epping Forest',
James Pollard, 1820, aquatint. Yale Center for British Art.

THE WILD-FLOWER NOSEGAY.

[Stanzas 1–6]

In life's first years as on a mother's breast,
    When Nature nurs'd me in her flowery pride,
I cull'd her bounty, such as seemed best,
    And made my garlands by some hedge-row side:
With pleasing eagerness the mind reclaims
    From black oblivion's shroud such artless scenes,
And cons the calendar of childish names
    With simple joy, when manhood intervenes.

From the sweet time that spring's young thrills are born,
    And golden catkins deck the sallow tree,
Till summer's blue-caps blossom mid the corn,
    And autumn's ragwort yellows o'er the lea,
I roam'd the fields about, a happy child,
    And bound my posies up with rushy ties,
And laugh'd and mutter'd o'er my visions wild,
    Bred in the brain of pleasure's ecstacies.

Crimp-frilled daisy, bright bronze buttercup,
    Freckt cowslip-peeps, gilt whins of morning's dew,
And hooded arum early sprouting up
    Ere the white-thorn bud half unfolds to view,
And wan-hued lady smocks, that love to spring
    'Side the swamp margin of some plashy pond;
And all the blooms that early Aprils bring,
    With eager joy each fill'd my playful hand:

The jaundice-tinctur'd primrose, sickly sere,
    Mid its broad curled leaves of mellow green,
Hemm'd in with relics of the 'parted year,
    The mournful wrecks of summers that have been—
Dead leaves of ash, and oak, and hazel tree,
    The constant covering of all woody land;
With tiny violets, creeping plenteously,
    That one by one entic'd my patient hand.

As shadowy April's suns and showers did pass,
    And summer's wild profusions plenteous grew,
Hiding the spring-flowers in long weeds and grass,
    What meads and copses would I wander thro'!
When on the water op'd the lily buds,

And fine long purples shadow'd in the lake,
When purple bugles peeped in the woods
   'Neath darkest shades that boughs and leaves could make.

Then did I wear day's many hours away
   In gathering blooms of seemly sweetest kinds,
Scrambling for blossoms of the white-thorn May,
   Ere they fell victims to unfeeling winds;
And twisted woodbines, and the flusht briar rose,
   How sweet remembrance on the mind doth rise
As they bow'd arching where the runnel flows,
   To think how oft I waded for the prize.

Erin Lafford

When John Clare sent 'The Wild-Flower Nosegay' to James Hessey and John Taylor in 1820, he was at once anxious for their approval and unapologetic about his theme. He states 'I am anxious that it shoud meet your opinion' and pleads 'If you like this *honestly tell me* the first oppertunity', before declaring 'I think vulgar names to the flowers best [...] but I know no others   if it pleases twill add a fresh spark to my ryhming pride' (*Letters*, pp. 104-7). 'The Wild-Flower Nosegay' is one of the most vivid examples of Clare's particular botanical allegiances and the important place plants hold in his dedication to the common and the 'vulgar'. Poetry, plants, and their blooms are closely entwined in Clare's imagination, where 'poesy' and 'posie' are always close echoes and allies. A nosegay is a small bouquet of flowers and herbs, chosen for their sweet smell and ornamental appeal, and often given as a gift. Its purpose is to delight and to give pleasure, but it can also distract from more unpleasant odours. The word itself is a compound of 'nose' and 'gay', and carries the various Middle English senses of its latter half, especially a bright or showy ornament to amuse a child, a trifle or whim, and the emotional state of joy or cheerfulness. Clare draws on these senses knowingly in this poem, which gathers and catalogues not only the abundance of wild flowers that grow in his local haunts, but also the childhood joys and freedoms associated with them. Clare's speaker follows his whims and leads us erratically along the 'hedge-row side', wanders through 'meads and copses' and into 'darkest shades', and stops at 'bushy bordering spots', tracing a landscape of memory in immediate and arresting detail. The poem is rich and alive with the common names of flowers, from 'blue-caps' and 'cowslip-peeps' to 'wan-hued lady smocks', 'ragged-robins', 'cuckoo-bud', and 'old-man's beard'. Clare clearly revels in the 'ryhming pride' and associative language these names offer him.

Yet, for all of its abundance of flowers and of joy, this poetic nosegay is not simply the cheerful trifle it advertises itself to be. The stanzas I've picked out for printing here exemplify, I think, the poem's elegiac undertone. Just as Clare's surefooted statement about his aesthetic choices is mingled with anxiety and vulnerability regarding this poem in his letter to his editors, so are the childhood nosegays he recalls framed as precarious gifts. The poem has much to say about the fleeting nature of childhood and its pleasures, how they can be as ephemeral as the 'tiny violets' that bloom amidst the 'constant' presence of woodland decay. At the same time, it stands as a careful testimony to their existence, and to poetry as a means of resurrecting joyful memories through a common botanical language. Clare may have worried about his editors' opinions, but he also sent the poem sensing 'that it woud give you pleasure likewise' (*Letters*, p. 104), crafting his own bittersweet nosegay in verse.

'Woodcutters at Park Place, Henley,
the River Thames Beyond', William Havell (1782–1857), c. 1826,
graphite and watercolour. The Metropolitan Museum of Art, New York.

WRITTEN IN AUTUMN.

(SONNET IX)

Checq'd Autumn, doubly sweet is thy declining,
  To meditate within this 'wilder'd shade;
To view the wood in its pied lustre shining,
  And catch thy varied beauties as they fade;
Where o'er broad hazel-leaves thy pencil mellows,
  Red as the glow that morning's opening warms,
And ash or maple 'neath thy colour yellows,
  Robbing some sunbeam of its setting charms:
I would say much of what now meets my eye,
But beauties lose me in variety.
  O for the warmth of soul and 'witching measure,
Expressing semblance, Poesy, which is thine,
  And Genius' eye to view this transient treasure,
That Autumn here might lastingly decline.

Sarah Zimmerman

Some of Clare's most striking innovations come from invoking poetic conventions and then pointedly abandoning them. 'Written in Autumn' conjures the sonnet's associations with a desire to immortalize a beloved in verse, in this case a 'declining' season. Just after the opening octave, however, the rhyme scheme breaks, and in a final, unconventional quatrain, the speaker relinquishes his aspirations with a sigh: 'O for the warmth of soul and 'witching measure, / Expressing semblance, Poesy, which is thine'. By this point, however, 'Autumn' has already been captured, not by the poet, but by the season itself, which has sketched 'the wood' with its own 'pencil'. The speaker longs for 'Genius' eye to view this transient treasure', but finds himself unable to 'say much of what now meets my eye' as seasonal 'beauties lose [him] in variety'. He is lost 'within this 'wilder'd shade', bewildered, and thereby finds himself, along with his natural environment, 'Written in Autumn', in an unconventional version of poetic immortality.

Beginning with its title, the poem contains multiple references to inscription. While the speaker remains content '[t]o meditate', autumn's pencil actively 'mellows' the 'broad hazel-leaves' and 'yellows' the 'ash or maple'. The 'sunbeam' is figured as a competing writing instrument temporarily '[r]obbed' of its 'setting charms' by a season awash in crimson and gold. John Taylor introduced Clare to the public by praising his ability to capture 'the light, and shade, and mezzotint of a landscape' (*Poems Descriptive*, p. xix). Here the term 'mezzotint' most obviously describes a middle tone, but it also invokes a kind of intaglio engraving in which 'subtle gradations of light and shade, rather than lines, form the image'.[1] With its description of a

'[c]hecq'd Autumn', 'the wood in its pied lustre shining', and 'varied beauties' that continually 'fade', Clare's opening octave seems to engrave the poet 'within this 'wilder'd shade'. Taylor reminds us in his 'Introduction' to *The Village Minstrel* that Clare's dreams of poetic immortality took print form from the beginning, quoting Clare on how 'by hard working, day and night, I at last got my one pound saved, for the printing of the proposals, which I never lost sight of' (1, p. ix). It is worth recalling that this collection featured Edward Scriven's stipple engraving of William Hilton's portrait of Clare.[2]

As the poet imagines it, 'Autumn' has engraved him in a dappled grove, where he and it 'might lastingly decline' together. 'Written in Autumn' thereby offers a double fantasy of inscribing in print form what Jane Bennett calls 'a more ecological sensibility'. Instead of a conventional scenario with a poet sketching the season, 'Autumn' wields the 'pencil' in a reversal of perspective that reflects 'the material agency or effectivity of nonhuman or not-quite-human things'. Resisting a traditional impulse to personify the season, Clare disperses agency throughout a leafy scene with continually shifting light that reflects 'a vibrant materiality that runs alongside and inside humans'.[3] The sonnet defines a distinctly Clarean ekphrasis that 'lastingly' locates the poet 'within the 'wilder'd shade' of his beloved Northamptonshire.

1   Elizabeth E. Barker, 'The Printed Image in the West: Mezzotint', *Heilbrunn Timeline of Art History* (New York: The Metropolitan Museum of Art), <http://www.metmuseum.org/toah/hd/mztn/hd_mztn.htm> (October 2003), [accessed 1 May 2021].

2   See the National Portrait Gallery's description: <https://www.npg.org.uk/collections/search/portrait/mw39576/John-Clare> [accessed 1 May 2021].

3   Jane Bennett, *Vibrant Matter: A Political Ecology of Things* (Durham: Duke University Press, 2010), pp. 10, ix, viii.

TO AN HOUR-GLASS

(SONNET XIV)

Old-fashioned uncouth measurer of the day,
   I love to watch thy filtering burthen pass;
Though some there are that live would bid thee stay;
   But these view reasons through a different glass
From him, Time's meter, who addresses thee.
   The world has joys which they may deem as such;
The world has wealth to season vanity,
   And wealth is theirs to make their vainness much:
But small to do with joys and Fortune's fee
Hath he, Time's chronicler, who welcomes thee.
   So jog thou on, through hours of doom'd distress;
So haste thou on the glimpse of hopes to come;
   As every sand-grain counts a trouble less,
As every drain'd glass leaves me nearer home.

Bridget Keegan

Clare's poetry tells time. 'To an Hour-glass' is one of many poems in *The Village Minstrel* referencing time in its title or content, whether clock, calendar or natural time. 'The Woodcutter's Evening Walk', 'Rural Morning', 'Sunday Walks', 'The Last of March', 'Written in Autumn', 'Daybreak', 'Noon'. Most of his sonnets have temporal indications in their titles and explicitly evoke time-awareness. Clare's perspective as a naturalist inspires him to describe nature at particular moments, offering specificity and accuracy. 'To an Hour-glass', however, is one of two sonnets devoted to the notion of time itself (the other being 'Time'). By the nineteenth century an hourglass was one of several instruments for measuring time in the everyday life of a villager, and Clare's fellow villagers would have understood multiple and complex temporal orders. Their relationship with time was not simply 'natural'— driven by the sun and the seasons. The calendar, months, days and hours were measured in ways well beyond those ordained by the church calendar or agricultural cycle. Not only are singular and transformational temporal occasions memorialised in Clare's poems, (events that might be categorised as 'kairos' time), Clare also attends to the passing of regular, abstract or 'chronos' time.

'To an Hourglass' opens with an apostrophe: 'Old-fashioned uncouth measurer of day'. By the 1820s the homes of labourers like Clare might have possessed a clock or watch. The hourglass, then, was already archaic. Nevertheless, like clocks it represented the imposition of abstract temporal regularity and order. Clare often portrayed himself as resistant to temporal impositions, slipping off on the Sabbath to wander the woods, for example. Yet instead of expressing disdain for an instrument that imposed time-consciousness on him, in the second line he asserts, 'I love to watch thy filtering burdens pass'. Clare most often employs the phrase 'I love' to introduce observations of natural phenomena, scenes from childhood or the past. His poems often convey nostalgia. Yet here he admires, even enthuses about the passage of time. Addressing the hourglass, he does not 'bid thee stay'. Instead, Clare identifies the desire to halt time as one experienced by the affluent. Time is money. Not having the latter, he is less concerned about losing the former. As 'Time's chronicler' the hourglass signals 'hopes to come' and the passing of 'hours of doom'd distress'. The poem ends with the speaker yearning for home. But this nostalgic ache is for once located in a future symbolised by the movement of sand through the glass.

His innovative descriptions of nature and profound local attachments identify Clare as a poet of place. But he is also a sophisticated chronicler of time. The temporalities in 'To an Hourglass' are not simply those of older rural culture. E. P. Thompson uses labouring-class poetry to show how time becomes an instrument of alienating work-discipline under industrial capitalism. However, Clare's portrayal of time as a source of consolation and hope warns us against simplifying the intellectual and emotional experience of labouring-class poets like Clare.

TO THE IVY

(SONNET XVII)

Dark creeping Ivy, with thy berries brown,
    That fondly twists' on ruins all thine own,
Old spire-points studding with a leafy crown
    Which every minute threatens to dethrone;
With fearful eye I view thy height sublime,
    And oft with quicker step retreat from thence
Where thou, in weak defiance, striv'st with Time,
    And holdst his weapons in a dread suspense.
But, bloom of ruins, thou art dear to me,
    When, far from danger's way, thy gloomy pride
Wreathes picturesque around some ancient tree
    That bows his branches by some fountain-side:
Then sweet it is from summer suns to be,
With thy green darkness overshadowing me.

James C. McKusick

John Clare's sonnet 'To the Ivy' opens with a meditation on the presence of 'dark creeping ivy' growing on ancient ruins. The ivy 'twists' all the way to the top of 'spire-points' and adorns them with a 'leafy crown', but the ivy also acts as an agent of decay, threatening to topple the ruined towers down onto the protagonist of the poem. Beating a quick retreat, the poet observes the ivy from a safer distance, and his slight frisson of terror renders the entire experience 'sublime', implicitly invoking Edmund Burke's concept of the sublime as something that threatens to destroy us. However, the role of the ivy is not inherently threatening; rather, it is one of 'weak defiance' as the ivy strives against time. Clare is hinting at the possibility that the ivy might actually be immortal, or unimaginably old, and thus able to survive far into the future when the ruin that it inhabits has decayed entirely into dust. Time holds no terrors for the ivy, since its branching network of vines will always be resilient in the face of loss and destruction. The sonnet's opening octave invokes the traditional aesthetic of the sublime only to repudiate its terror, and it commends the ivy's resilience in defiance of time.

    The sonnet's final sestet affirms the poet's enduring affection for the ivy, hailing it as the 'bloom of ruins' and envisioning its growth as 'picturesque' as it wreathes around an ancient tree. The term 'picturesque' connotes a more placid and appealing aspect of the natural world, one that welcomes the protagonist and offers him a quiet nook, shaded from the summer sun. The most charismatic figure in the poem's last six lines is undoubtedly the ancient tree 'that bows his branches by some fountain-side', and the tree would surely be the centre of attention in a conventional painting of this scene. But Clare is far from conventional in his depiction of the rural landscape, and by focusing on the ivy, he decentres the attention of the reader. The ivy is an exemplar of Clare's rhizomatic vision.

The liminal role of the ivy is most vividly evoked in the poem's closing couplet: 'Then sweet it is from summer suns to be, / With thy green darkness overshadowing me'. The ivy provides a shady spot where the poet can simply be. The infinitive verb 'to be' expresses the poet's desire to dwell within a branching network of living tendrils that shelter him from the summer sun. The ivy overshadows him with a 'green darkness' that is comforting and protective, offering a moment of cool stasis in a larger world still subject to the ravages of time. The poem's final rhyme of 'be' with 'me' emphasizes the existential quality of the dwelling-in-place afforded by the ivy. An uncharismatic dark-green plant reveals an unexpected depth of meaning in this simple, yet profound poem.

WINTER.

.... but wanders on
From hill to dale, still more and more astray:
Impatient flouncing through the drifted heaps,
Stung with the thoughts of home........

WINTER

(SONNET XXXV)

The small wind whispers through the leafless hedge
    Most sharp and chill, where the light snowy flakes
Rest on each twig and spike of wither'd sedge,
    Resembling scatter'd feathers;— vainly breaks
The pale split sunbeam through the frowning cloud,
    On Winter's frowns below— from day to day
Unmelted still he spreads his hoary shroud,
    In dithering pride on the pale traveller's way,
Who, croodling, hastens from the storm behind
Fast gathering deep and black, again to find
    His cottage-fire and corner's sheltering bounds;
Where, haply, such uncomfortable days
    Make musical the wood-sap's frizzling sounds,
And hoarse loud bellows puffing up the blaze.

Fiona Stafford

During the coldest months of the year, the wind rarely remains small for very long. Although Clare's soft, alliterative opening may evoke a gentle breeze, 'Winter' is echoing in the 'wind' and its 'whispers', carrying a warning of stronger blasts to come. Though 'small', this wind is already powerful enough to disrupt the iambs with a spondaic gust, picked up in the next line with 'Most sharp'. The simple words gather force through acoustic suggestion: a wind both 'sharp' and 'chill' must surely be shrill. The sense of an imminent blizzard hangs over the poem like a 'frowning cloud', uneasiness gathering 'deep and black' towards the inevitable. The coming storm is just the latest blow dealt by omnipotent 'Winter'.

Hard, cold fields are starved of life. The 'leafless hedge' offers little shelter to birds, whose familiar perches are covered in snow. Clare's carefully observed details conjure absence rather than presence. 'Wither'd sedge' broken by heavy wind and snow, heads collapsing in all directions, 'Resembling scatter'd feathers', recalls the birds no longer there. Whether prey to the hungry, sport for the better-fed, or victims of months when water turns ice-solid and food supplies run short, the summer inhabitants of long grasses and green hedgerows have left behind only feathers. A prolonged cold spell, 'from day to day / Unmelted' takes its toll. Even the sun seems powerless to ward off winter's 'hoary shroud'. All colour drains from the landscape as dark and light form an unholy alliance of storm-cloud and snow. When life finally enters the poem in the shape of a 'pale traveller', the country from whose 'bourn' none returns seems all too close at hand.

For those lost in a blizzard, a cloud can become a shroud soon enough. As deep drifts obscure local features, the dangers intensify. Clare's sonnet gathers strength from the tradition of 'winter' poems depicting its unluckiest victims. Among the well-known images in Thomson's 'Winter' (illustrated by Bewick and Stothard, 1805 edition, see p. 26) is the farm worker who loses his way in heavy snow at nightfall, 'down he sinks, beneath the shelter of a shapeless drift'. While his wife and children wait anxiously at home, he freezes to death in a nearby field transformed utterly by winter's hoary shroud.

If Clare's sonnet builds anticipations of quiet catastrophe and related moralising, it suddenly takes an unexpected turn. The octave's regular Shakespearean rhymes are followed by an apparently closing couplet, but instead the traveller reaches 'His cottage fire', setting off another quatrain. In defiance of winter's frown, he has been 'croodling' to combat the cold and poetic convention. Starved winter branches are now transformed into frizzling wood-sap, chill winds blasted out by 'Hoarse, loud bellows' even more capable of challenging winter's relentless iambs than the 'small wind'. Clare had no need of an Aeolian harp – winter's winds worked just as well, their chill whispers answered by the unlikely corresponding chords of spitting logs and coughing bellows. Inside a warm cottage, imagination blazes, stoked by the sounds of home and hearth.

ELIZA EMMERSON READS
THE VILLAGE MINSTREL

Jonathan Bate

John Clare fandom may be said to have begun with Eliza Emmerson. As I demonstrated in my biography, her letters to him are among the most intimate that we have; the loss of his to her is perhaps the biggest gap in the story of his life. There is, accordingly, special serendipity in the rediscovery of her annotated copy of the second volume of *The Village Minstrel* in the year of its bicentenary.[1] Her comments are of double value in their combination of personal details and responses that are representative of the ways in which Clare's early work was read at the moment of publication.

A full transcription is given here.[2] Though there are instances that may sound like condescension ('Here is depth of reflection from a <u>Peasant</u>'), there is also praise that is both fulsome and astute. Among the most interesting observations are the frequent suggestions that Clare's poems are painterly, and indeed that they provide images which could be rendered into delightful genre scenes by Eliza Emmerson's other protégé, the artist E. V. Rippingille; the apt comparison with other poets (the ballad 'Winter's gone' compared to a pastoral of Sir Walter Raleigh, 'Woman' as worthy of Byron or Tom Moore, the sonnet on 'Night' truly Shakespearean); and the recognition of Clare's sheer range, from 'playfulness' to 'romantic Sublimity'. 'E-L-E', as she signs many of the annotations, clearly took deep joy in her friendship with Clare—and particular pride in the fact that, as she reveals here, 'To the Rural Muse', one of his signature poems (placed at the climax of the 'Poems', prior

---

1   Forum Auctions, 25 March 2021, Lot 148 <https://bit.ly/35OAje5> [accessed 19 June 2021]: a complete set of Clare's published volumes, all of them bearing the bookplate of E. Goodfellow of Helpston (member of a farming family still active in the area); alone in the set, volume 2 of *The Village Minstrel* has copious pencil annotations in the hand of Eliza Emmerson. The Goodfellows owned Clare's Helpston cottage, so Emmerson's intention was probably for them to pass the annotations on to him, which would explain her frequent use of 'you'. I am most grateful to the purchaser for sharing the volume with me and allowing me to publish these transcriptions.

2   With the exception of a handful of local comments on possible misprints or curious phrasings, and of 'x' markings against many of the titles and many lines that she considered especially felicitous.

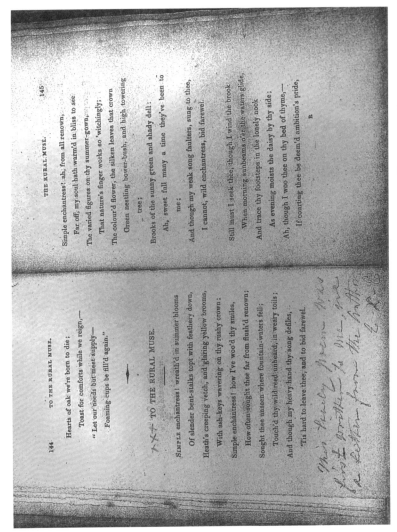

144   TO THE RURAL MUSE.

Hearts of oak we're born to die;
    Toast for comforts while we reign,—
"Let our needs but meet supply—
    Foaming cups be fill'd again."

TO THE RURAL MUSE.

SIMPLE enchantress! wreath'd in summer blooms
Of slender bent-stalks topt with feathery down,
Heath's creeping vetch, and glaring yellow brooms,
With ash-keys wavering on thy rushy crown;
Simple enchantress! how I've woo'd thy smiles,
How often sought thee far from flush'd renown;
Sought thee unseen where fountain-waters fell;
Touch'd thy wild reed unheard, in weary toils;
And though my heavy hand thy song defiles,
'Tis hard to leave thee, and to bid farewel.

THE RURAL MUSE.   145

Simple enchantress! ah, from all renown,
Far off, my soul hath warm'd in bliss to see
The varied figures on thy summer-gown,
That nature's finger works so 'witchingly;
The colour'd flower, the silken leaves that crown
Green nestling bower-bush, and high towering
    tree;
Brooks of the sunny green and shady dell:
Ah, sweet full many a time they've been to
    me;
And though my weak song faulters, sung to thee,
I cannot, wild enchantress, bid farewel.

Still must I seek thee, though I wind the brook
When morning sunbeams o'er the waters glide,
And trace thy footsteps in the lonely nook
As evening moists the daisy by thy side;
Ah, though I woo thee on thy bed of thyme,—
If courting thee be deem'd ambition's pride,

B

Sample of Eliza Emmerson's annotations to *The Village Minstrel* to the sequence of 'Sonnets'), 'was first written to me, in a letter, from the Author'.

'Rosy Jane': the line 'Thus Jane sat milking, full of thought' is marked and at the foot of the page Emmerson writes 'Another subject for Rip?' (she also places a + next to the line 'His jacket shone so red, so gay').

'Childish Recollections': 'I cannot read this sweet poem without having the simple and interesting Author before my eyes, such as he really is—All Nature & Simplicity!'

'The Woodman': 'This poem has some very lovely passages in it'. The stanza that begins

> The woodman smokes, the brats in mirth and glee,
> And artless prattle, even's hours beguile,
> While love's last pledge runs scrambling up his knee...

is marked out, with the comment 'This, would make a lovely subject for a picture'.

'Impromptu': 'Oh, what sweetness, what simplicity and tenderness in this little Poem'.

'Ballad' ('Winter's gone'): 'This poem is full of sweet <u>pastoral</u> feeling—and is little (if any) inferior to the beautiful Pastoral of "Phillida & Coridon" by Sir Walter Raleigh'.

'Narrative Verses': Clare's hope that future days would 'grant to me a crown of bays' is underlined and at the foot of the page Emmerson writes 'a never fading one <u>is thine</u>, cull'd from Nature's most simple, and sweetest flowers!'

'Song of Praise': 'This is sublime, and truly beautiful!'

'To the Butterfly': on the first page, 'Hope is cast of liberty', and later, 'Who could have written more fully and sweetly on this simple subject? Not any one!'

'Rural Morning': 'What a lovely picture is this of <u>pastoral beauty</u>'.

'Rural Evening': The lines beginning

> At even's hour, the truce of toil, 'tis sweet
> The sons of labour at their ease to meet,
> On piled bench, beside the cottage door...

are marked, and Emmerson comments, 'This would give an excellent subject to our friend "<u>Rip</u>" for a <u>picture</u>'. Later in the poem, the image of these 'sons of labour' lighting their pipes and chatting about wages and local gossip elicits 'a charming group might be made from this—for the <u>picture</u>! E-L-E'.

'The Cross Roads': 'This poem is full of truth, simplicity, and pathos, and in parts equal to any thing I ever read. E-L-E'.

'Sunday Walks': 'This is a lovely and philosophic poem'.

'The Cress-Gatherer': 'The opening of this poem is very sweet'.

'Man's Mortality': 'It may be truly said of Clare that he can go "from gay to Grave—from lively to severe"—' [quoting a line from Pope's 'Essay on Man', with 'grave to gay' inverted].

'To the Right Honorable Admiral Lord Radstock': 'Too much cannot be said on this subject by you, to your noble and excellent Patron—to whom you owe eternal obligations'.

'The Wild-Flower Nosegay': 'This "Nosegay" has the very essence of true Poesy—E L E'. 'What painting is here!', she exclaims with regard to one of the best and most characteristic stanzas:

> And down the hay-fields, wading 'bove the knees
>> Through seas of waving grass, what days I've gone,
> Cheating the hopes of many labouring bees
>> By cropping blossoms they were perch'd upon;
> As thyme along the hills, and lambtoe knots,
>> And the wild stalking Canterbury bell,
> By hedge-row side or bushy bordering spots,
>> That loves in shade and solitude to dwell.

Song ('There was a time'): 'Full of delicate tenderness and reflection'.

Song ('There's the daisy'): 'What poesy—what playfulness!'

'To the Rural Muse' [triple 'x' marking against the title]: 'This lovely poem was first written to me, in a letter, from the Author E-L-E'.

'Home': 'There is in this sonnet what must come home to every bosom'.

'The Tomb': 'What a mixture of harshness and beauty is here'.

'Sorrows for a friend': 'This sonnet is full of melancholy sweetness, and tender reflection'.

'To my cottage': 'The same feeling will exist—be thy future fortune what it may!'

'Poverty': 'These are past—and may such miseries never more be thine! E-L-E'.

'To my Mother': 'Who would not help and love such a one otherwise'.

'The Snowdrop': 'How beautiful—how true!'

'Life': 'I should have considered this sonnet as written a century ago from the style'.

'Written in Autumn': 'Would that you could use your <u>pencil</u> as you do your <u>pen</u>!'

'On Death': 'Without meaning to be ungrateful—I would join in the same wish my friend! E-L-E'.

'Native Scenes': 'How every line comes home to the heart! ELE'.

'Peace': 'Here is excellent philosophy—and great <u>truth</u>!'

'Morning': 'Thou art indeed the inspired Poet of Nature my dear friend!—E-L-E

'To an Hour-Glass': 'Clare proves himself in this to be a man of deep reflection'.

'To an Angry Bee': 'How playful and tender is this'.

'Day-break': 'What a lovely <u>picture</u> in this—of early morn'.

'To the Ivy': 'There is a romantic Sublimity in this Sonnet'.

'Hope': 'How blithely treated and yet how serious!'

'Nature': 'I have known these feelings from my very childhood—ELE'.

'A Wish': 'How natural—what spot so dear as home ever to repose our <u>Ashes</u>'.

'Hereafter': 'Full of calm Christian feeling—I think like you my dear Clare—E-L-E'.

'The Ants': 'Full of observation and reflection'.

'Milton Abbey': 'This breathes a high feeling of Gratitude in Clare to his noble benefactor Ld Milton'.

'Night': 'This is truly Shakesperean [sic]'.

'Noon': 'How full of sweetness and tenderness!'

'Autumn': 'Truly <u>fine</u> and <u>poetical</u>'.

'To Time': 'Here is depth of reflection from a <u>Peasant</u>'.

'Twilight': 'It is truly astonishing to see how Clare combines <u>painting</u> with poesy!'

'Expression': 'This sonnet classed with "Taste" and "Envy"—each of them very fine!'

'Woman': 'Worthy of Byron or Moore'.

'Summer Tints': 'This is Poetry and painting!'

'Wild Nosegay': 'How airy and playful is this sonnet—it is a "Wild-Nosegay"'.

'On Taste': 'An astonishing effort this—for such a man as Clare!'

'May-Noon': 'Full of lonely, and sweet feeling!'

'To ****' [on envy]: 'Nothing can exceed the beauty with which Clare has <u>adorn'd</u> this <u>ugly subject</u>!'

'To Autumn': 'Though last, not the least beautiful! E-L-E'.

'Barking Timber in Wychwood Forest, Oxfordshire' by Joshua Cristall,
c. 1818. The Metropolitan Museum of Art, New York.

John Clare's Contemporaries: The Anonymous Versifier

Nic Wilson

A Poetical Tribute of Respect to John Clare, the Northamptonshire Poet

Hail! Pleasing Poet; though distrest, and poor,
Thy richer Genius Nature can display;
And though unskill'd in deep and classick lore,
Her varied Beauties faithfully portray.

Creation's Wonders, though minute and small,
Are open to thy fond research and view;
With microscopic eye thou scann'st them all,
And giv'st thy praises, where the praise is due.

Whene'er, to leave this earth thy warning's giv'n,
(Her pure, rich joys, thy still exhaustless mine;)
O may the purer, richer joys of Heav'n,
Through all Eternity, O Clare, be thine.

JWN 28 March 1821[1]

Hundreds of letters sent to John Clare between 1818 and 1851 are collected in six weighty volumes in the manuscript archives of the British Library. Late one afternoon, as I scoured the early letters under the spotlight, a short letter caught my eye: a single poem dedicated to Clare, sent from my home town, Hitchin, on 28 March 1821.[2] This unattributed letter, categorised by Mark Storey in *The Critical Heritage* as 'author not known', is signed only with a flourish of initials.[3] I was intrigued by this mystery. Who had written to Clare from Hitchin and why in the form of a poetical tribute?

The signature looks a little like JM, or perhaps JWN. From the ranks of notable figures in Hitchin in the 1820s, only one man fits the possible initials – Joseph White Niblock – a stipendiary curate of St Mary's Church, Hitchin, a Classics scholar and Master of the local Free School from 1819 to 1830. Was this Hitchin curate the phantom verse writer? Did he compose the tribute after reading *Poems Descriptive of Rural Life and Scenery*, picking up his pen (or possibly, comparing the formal calligraphy with his other rather illegible letters, instructing one of his pupils to transcribe the poem) and claiming it only with his initials? The letter has no address so it seems unlikely that it would have been sent through the post. Perhaps it accompanied a parcel or was delivered by a mutual acquaintance – maybe even by the writer himself?

Joseph White Niblock seems, at first sight, to be an unlikely candidate to have written to a 'distrest and poor' poet.[4] Born in 1786 and baptised in the Independent Congregational Chapel in Liverpool, Joseph was the oldest son of James and Elizabeth Niblock (née Parkin).[5] He graduated with a BA from St Edmund's College, Oxford in 1808 and married Christiana Spenser, daughter of the Rev. Edward Spencer, in St John's Church, Hackney in 1811.[6] In the same year, Joseph was ordained as a deacon in Buckden, St Neots and by 1812 he had been ordained as a priest. He went on to serve as a stipendiary curate in Bletsoe, Riseley and Melchbourne (all in north Bedfordshire) from 1811 to 1815, before moving twenty miles south to Hitchin in September 1817.[7] His stipend was £50 annually with surplice fees, Easter offerings and the use of a house.[8]

In 1819, Niblock took up the post of Master of the Free School alongside his church duties and gained a reputation as an exacting Classics scholar who complained about teaching the 'miserable relics' of his predecessor's misrule.[9] Local dignitaries were pleased to have a master in post who had produced a Latin dictionary and was, at heart, a Classics man – important in a town where Latin had been taught since at least the 1630s.[10] Niblock's lack of sympathy with the poor boys he taught is often cited in Hitchin's historic accounts, with Robert Walmsley quoting the schoolmaster's statement that he found it 'easier to teach two hundred bright scholars than the twenty-one (!) miserable specimens left by my predecessor, nine of whom cannot read'.[11] Another local historian, Joyce Donald, claimed Niblock was 'reputed to be one of the best Greek scholars in England, and certainly more Greek was studied in his time than at any other. A Greek Grammar which he wrote was used at Eton and other public schools for many years'.[12]

Niblock appeared in various records in the 1820s and 30s. He subscribed to religious tracts, poetry collections and the Rev. J.

Bull's sermons (the curate of Clipston in Northamptonshire and master of the local Endowed Grammar School and Hospital).[13] His ecclesiastical role involved proving last wills and testaments, performing burial ceremonies and writing letters to the Home Secretary on behalf of parishioners and prisoners, such as the seventeen-year-old Joseph South, and later George Hide and James Watson, vouching for their good characters and requesting leniency in the face of the death penalty.[14] Niblock signed the letter to the Home Secretary, Sir Robert Peel, in defence of George Hide, 'Your most obedient and devoted servant, Joseph White Niblock, D.D., Hitchin, Herts'.[15] The handwriting of this signature matches the initials at the end of the poem to Clare, revealing the letters to be JWN and confirming Niblock as the unknown correspondent.

Initials at the end of the anonymous letter to Clare.
© British Library Board Egerton 2245 f306r

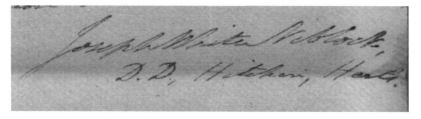

Niblock's signature on his letter to the Home Secretary.
Reproduced by kind permission of the National Archives

So why might this schoolmaster and clergyman have been inspired to write to Clare? Niblock would seem from his Anglican training and Classical education to have come from a vastly different background to the Northamptonshire poet, but information in the Home Office archives, genealogical records and newspaper articles suggests that there were more similarities between the two men than might immediately be apparent. Joyce Donald's introduction to Niblock states that 'born the son of a poor draper in Bath, he so impressed the Low Church Party of the city that they assisted him to St. Edmund's Hall, Oxford, where he took Holy Orders'.[16] Her reference to the family's poverty contradicts the description of Joseph's father as a 'gent' in the *Alumni Oxoniensis* (1715-1886):

> Niblock, Joseph White, s. James, of Liverpool, Lancashire, gent. St Edmund Hall, matric. 2 May, 1808, aged 21; B.A. 1812, M.A. 1824, B.D. 1825, D.D. 1825 [...][17]

James Niblock's enigmatic life and career is central to understanding his son's aspirations and abilities. James was born in Stranraer, Scotland in 1763, son of a horse setter (a man who hired out horses).[18] The first indication of James' profession was in the *Leeds Intelligencer* in 1786 which referred to 'one 20l. Bill drawn by Thomas Varley of Linguards on James Niblock, Merchant, Liverpool'.[19] He was listed in 1788 in the *Manchester Mercury* under 'Goods for Sale 'Goods for Sale "General Commission Repository" James Niblock and Joseph White, No. 41 Whitechapel, Liverpool'.[20] This reference suggests that the namesake of his eldest son was his business partner Joseph White, most likely a mariner in Liverpool.[21] James appeared again in 1790 when his friend Mr George Latham of Birmingham (another of his partners) died at his house in Liverpool and a year later, when he was listed in *The Bath Chronicle and Weekly Gazette* as bankrupt: 'James Niblock and William Hunter (late) of Liverpool, Linen Drapers'.[22] These records indicate that James was trading in linen (and later wool) and other goods, possibly brought into Liverpool from Stranraer and Ireland.

By 1795, James was a merchant tradesman at No 1. Street, Bristol (under the name Niblock and Hunter); then from 1797-99 he was listed at 19 Bridge Street, Bristol as 'Niblock and Burgess': 'commission brokers, financial services, auctioneers, repository, storage, warehouse, commerce'.[23] 'Niblock, J. and Burgess, G. Bristol, Linen Drapers' appeared again in 1800 in the bankruptcy

1795 halfpenny token © The Fitzwilliam Museum, Cambridge

lists and by 1811 he was partnered with Richard Stanley Latham (possibly a relation of George Latham) as a woollen draper in Bristol.[24] Niblock and Latham produced their own sixpence and shilling tokens in 1811, and this was not the first time James had addressed the scarcity and poor quality of coinage in this period by issuing tokens to promote the business in a challenge to the legal currency of the day. In an article in the *British Numismatic Journal*, James O'Donald Mays notes:

> Niblock and Latham conducted an auctioneering business from their 'Sales Room' at 18 Bridge Street, as well as a woollen drapery shop next door at no 19. It was their predecessor, Niblock and Hunter, which issued the famous halfpenny tokens in 1795 [...] portraying the two men in the midst of a conversation. The first said 'I want to buy some cheap bargains', to which the second replied, 'Then go to Niblock's in Bridge Street.' Niblock and Latham indicate on their token [...] that they also conducted business at Trowbridge'.[25]

Six of the halfpenny tokens and two of the shilling tokens are currently held in the coin collection at the Fitzwilliam Museum in Cambridge.

In 1822, the old story recurred when James became bankrupt again, advertising for sale his 'Public Sale Room, No 15 Lower Sackville Street'.[26] This enterprising merchant seems to have been talented at establishing businesses and making a success of them, if only for limited periods. He also had a more nefarious side, according to a report to the Home Office in 1804 in which the Mayor of Liverpool, John B. Aspinall, described an anonymous letter he had received hinting at a plot to blow up parliament. The man indicted in the letter was said to be travelling to England to stay with one James Niblock. The Mayor contacted the Home Office in concern, describing James as 'an Irishman and a general auctioneer, [who] had been well known in Liverpool and was now in Bristol'. Aspinall wrote:

> Having discovered that Niblock [...] is well known to have lived in Liverpool several years ago after having kept a shop for some time he failed and took up the Business of a general Auctioneer and the disposing of almost all kinds of Goods, such as Manchester, Sheffield + Birmingham Good and also Woollens and Linens, etc. etc. that he is an Irishman and that he and all his acquaintances were of very suspicious character – and I also learn that he himself is at this time in Bristol.[27]

That James Niblock, a non-conformist 'Irishman' from Stranraer where the dissenting chapels were well attended and many of the inhabitants spoke in a Scottish accent with a Galloway Irish brogue, was noted as being of 'very suspicious character' is extremely telling of attitudes towards nationality and religion in early-nineteenth-century England. Despite the Mayor of Liverpool's suspicions, James appears to have emerged from the scandal unscathed and by 1817, had established himself as a Freemason in the city of Bath.[28]

Joseph White Niblock may have been born into a poor, non-conformist, Irish-Scottish family, but his father clearly had gumption, intelligence and more than a dash of audacity. Joseph inherited his father's acuity, becoming a scholar, master and clergyman, and his youngest daughter, Amelia St. John Niblock, married Captain Hon. William Henry George Wellesley, nephew of the Duke of Wellington and a Dublin man from an old County Kildare family, in 1842.[29] The meteoric social rise of the Niblock family within two generations says much about their abilities and ambition. When the Honourable Amelia St John Wellesley died in 1889 in Switzerland, she left a personal estate of £19,615 1s. 1d.[30]

Despite being criticised in historical accounts for favouring his private pupils, there is also less well-studied documentation that suggests Niblock was keen to assist those less fortunate than himself. He was a supporter of the missionary cause and campaigned for the instigation of a school for poor girls. In 1817, Niblock set up a Penny Association in aid of the Bedfordshire Church Missionary Society in his parish of Riseley. The report in *The Missionary Register* states that 'Between forty and fifty persons, chiefly labourers and school-children, cheerfully subscribe their weekly pence'.[31] He continued to collect donations throughout his time in Bedfordshire and Hitchin. He also seconded a motion to establish a Hertfordshire Missionary Association in 1823 and preached a sermon on its anniversary the following year in Willian, a village near Hitchin.[32]

In the summer of 1818, Paternoster's Printers in Market Place, Hitchin, produced handbills announcing a 'general meeting' which led to the establishment of the British Schools Girls' School. The notices reveal that 'The Reverend J W Niblock of the Independent Church next door took the chair'.[33] It is interesting that he championed a school that admitted the 'female children of the poor of the town' of both 'Churchmen and Dissenters' and that he was described as being 'of the Independent Church'.[34] His wife, Christiana, also sat on the school committee, along with other women of all denominations.[35]

Niblock set up a Sunday School which met across the river from St Mary's (the Anglican Church where he was curate) in the poorest part of town 'in a room at Barnard's Yard in Dead Street' (the same street that housed the Independent Chapel meeting house from 1703-1844).[36] In 1823, a piece of plate was presented by 'the teachers of the Hitchin Church Sunday School to the Rev. Joseph White Niblock, B.A., as a small tribute of their gratitude for his unremitting attention to the interests of the school during the time he filled the office of president'.[37] Despite his position as an Anglican curate, it would seem that he maintained a connection with his Nonconformist roots throughout his time in Hitchin.

Given Niblock's religious and philanthropic interests, it seems likely that John Taylor's introduction to *Poems Descriptive of Rural Life and Scenery* would have appealed to him, perhaps as much as the content and quality of the poetry itself. Although not born into such extreme poverty as Clare, Niblock may well have identified with the younger man's desire to access learning above his station and better himself through literary pursuits. Niblock had been assisted in his own education by those wealthier than himself and had dedicated much of his life to 'the arduous and delightful task of instructing youth'.[38] Clare's dedication to taking on 'extra work as a ploughboy, and by helping his father morning and evening at threshing' to earn the money to pay for his education would, no doubt, have impressed Niblock who was more used to his own students skipping lessons so they could earn money in the fields.[39]

Perhaps Niblock also identified with Clare's desire to communicate through poetry. Were his own verses composed as a nod to Clare's work or as a way of displaying his own poetical aspirations? His tribute to the poet was not the only time he attempted to convey his message through iambic pentameter. In 1835, as editor of *The Textuary and Ritualist* (a guide for students of the Bible), he included his own poem 'How to Read the Bible' simply initialled 'JWN' at the end – a modest sleight of hand in a text whose editor is also hidden behind the attribution 'a clergyman'.[40] Taylor's account of Clare's early study of the Bible and his ability to repeat the third chapter of Job from memory would have impressed Niblock, who encouraged students in 'How to Read the Bible' to:

> Read it each morning early, and each eve;
> And as the *very word of God*, receive.
> Look for the blessed Jesus, *every where*;
> And mourn, if, in searching, you can't find him there.
> In *persons, places, things,* the Saviour see,
> Pourtray'd, to shadow forth his work *to thee*.[41]

In his tribute to Clare, Niblock praised the poet's ability to see the word of God in everything, noting 'Creation's Wonders, though minute and small, / Are open to thy fond research and view'.[42] These lines suggest that, in Niblock's view, Clare's genius for portraying natural beauty more than makes up for his lack of skill in 'deep and classick lore'.[43]

Both of Niblock's poems conclude with Christian redemption through death. He advised students:

> This if you do, and ever keep in mind,
> The Bible easy, pleasant, you will find;
> And, moulded by its soul-transforming pow'r,
> You shall be blest thro' life, and save'd in death's dark hour.[44]

Joseph White Niblock, from the Lawson Thompson Scrapbook.
Reproduced by kind permission of North Hertfordshire Museum Service

Niblock's wish for Clare to attain the 'purer, richer joys of Heav'n'
indicates that he believed the poet was already deserving of
salvation through his dedication to study, his 'microscopic eye'
and his knowledge of the Bible.[45] But there is also a sense in which
the final stanza of Niblock's tribute is a response to the ending of
'Helpstone', the opening poem in *Poems Descriptive of Rural Life
and Scenery*. This poem explores Clare's wish to end his life at
home, freed for eternity to wander the landscape of his childhood:

> Those charms of youth, that I again may see,
> May it be mine to meet my end in thee;
> And, as reward for all my troubles past,
> Find one hope true – to die at home at last![46]

In contrast, Niblock's vision for Clare leaves Helpston far behind:

> Whene'er, to leave this earth thy warning's giv'n,
> (Her pure, rich joys, thy still exhaustless mine;)
> O may the purer, richer joys of Heav'n,
> Through all Eternity, O Clare, be thine.[47]

Perhaps, for all his admiration of the poet's 'richer genius', Niblock couldn't resist the didactic temptation to provide Clare with a more conventional Christian ending.[48]

The truth about how Niblock's letter reached Clare without name or address, and why it was only signed with his initials, remains a mystery. If the poem was enclosed in a parcel or with a book, why was there no reference to the gift? If it was delivered by a mutual acquaintance, why was Clare's name not written on the back of the letter? Perhaps one sunny afternoon two centuries ago, Joseph White Niblock knocked at John Clare's cottage door, letter in hand. He had, after all, worked for several years in parishes just 30 miles south and was likely to have known many local clergymen and ministers like Isaiah Knowles Holland, a non-conformist friend of Clare's and another active supporter of the missionary cause. But this is all surmise. What we do know is that the letter with its tributary verses suggests that *Poems Descriptive of Rural Life and Scenery* had the power to touch the lives of educators and self-made men like the Rev. Joseph White Niblock, who admired Clare's poetic genius and his ability to express God's wonder through his depiction of the natural world, despite the manifest poverty and educational paucity of his upbringing.

NOTES

I am grateful to the Manuscript Department of the British Library and the National Archives, Kew for permission to quote from correspondence relating to James and Joseph White Niblock. With thanks to Dr Robert Heyes of the John Clare Society, Dr Martin Allen at the Fitzwilliam Museum and Malcolm Toogood, historian at Bath Masonic Hall.

1.   British Library, Egerton Manuscript (hereafter Eg.) 2245, fol. 306r.
2.   Ibid.
3.   *Critical Heritage*, p.59.
4.   Eg. 2245, fol. 306r.
5.   The National Archives (NA), *England and Wales Non-Conformist and Non-Parochial Registers, 1567-1970, Lancashire, Congregational, Piece 1045: Liverpool, Newington Chapel, Renshaw Street (Congregational), 1776-1808*, p.17.
6.   *Alumni Oxoniensis: The Members of the University of Oxford, 1715-1886*, 4 vols (Oxford; James Parker & co., ca. 1888-1891), III (1891), 1020 and London Metropolitan Archives, *London, England, Church of England Marriages and Banns, 1754-1932, Hackney, St. John, Hackney, 1804-1821*, p. 165.

7.   *Clergy of the Church of England Database*, CCEd Person ID: 71392, https://theclergydatabase.org.uk [accessed 7 June 2021].

8.   Ibid.; incorrectly recorded under the name Joshua White Niblock.

9.   Joyce Donald, *The John Mattocke Boys* (Hitchin: the author, 1990), p.16.

10. Ibid., see pp. 9-10.

11. Robert Walmsley, *Some Schools in Hitchin History* (Hitchin: Hitchin Historical Society, 1984), p. 11.

12. Donald, p.17.

13. *The Twenty-Fifth Annual Report of the Religious Tract Society* (London: P. White, 1824), p. 82; *The Jewel: Being Sacred, Domestic, Narrative, and Lyrical Poems*, ed. by Thomas Sloper (London: Richard Groombridge, 1839), p. 295 and Rev. J. Bull, *Sermons on the Fifty First Psalm* (London: Thomas Abbott, 1824), p. xi.

14. Hertfordshire Archives Local Studies (HALS), Will of Peter Moles, 23HR156; HALS, *Parish Register of St. Marys Church, Hitchin*, Register Entry No. 384; NA, HO 17/53/48 and HO 17/122/186.

15. NA, HO 17/122/186.

16. Donald, pp. 15-16.

17. *Alumni Oxoniensis*, 1020.

18. *Scotland Select Births and Baptisms, 1564-1960* and see *Stranraer Parish Roll of Baptisms, 1695-1773*, http://sites.rootsweb.com/~wghannay/stranraer-baptisms-07.html [accessed 7 June 2021].

19. *Leeds Intelligencer*, 7 November, 1786, 3.

20. *Manchester Mercury*, 22 April, 1788, 2.

21. Robert Craig and Rupert Jarvis, *Liverpool Registry of Merchant Ships* (Manchester: Chetham Society, 1967) p. 27.

22. *Chester Chronicle*, 19 March 1790, 4, and *Bath Chronicle and Weekly Gazette*, 11 August, 1791, 2.

23. William Matthews, *The Complete Bristol Directory* (Bristol: the author, 1797, 1798 and 1799).

24. *The Monthly Magazine or British Register* (London: R. Phillips, 1800) x, part II, 463.

25. James O'Donald Mays, 'Silver Tokens and Bristol', *British Numismatic Journal*, 48 (1978), 98-106 (102).

26. *Bristol Mirror*, 5 January, 1822, 2.

27. NA, Home Office, Domestic Correspondence, George III, HO 42, Letters and Papers, fols 145-147B (fol. 146).

28. *United Grand Lodge of England Freemason Membership Registers, 1751-1921, United Grand Lodge of England, 1813-1836, Register of Admissions: Country and Foreign*, p. 34.

29. *England and Wales, Civil Registration Marriage Index, 1837-1915*, Yorkshire West Riding, vol. 22, p. 401.

30. *England and Wales, National Probate Calendar* (Index of Wills and Administrations), 1858-1995 (1890), p. 46.

31. *The Missionary Register* (London: L.B. Seeley, 1817), p. 28.

32. *The Missionary Register* (London: L.B. Seeley, 1823), p. 535 and *The Missionary Register* (London: L.B. Seeley, 1824), p. 339.

33. *Educating our own: The Masters of the Hitchin Boys' British School 1810-1929* (Hitchin: Hitchin British Schools Trust, 2008), p. 26.

34. HALS 67519 – 67554, Reports of the British Schools (Girls), Dead Street, Hitchin.

35. HALS 67555, Minutes of the British Schools Hitchin.

36. Reginald Hine, *History of Hitchin*, 2 vols (Hitchin: Eric T. Moore, 1972), II, 104; first publ. (London: George Allen & Unwin, 1929).

37. *Annual Register or a View of the History and Politics of the Year* 1843 (London: F. & J. Rivington, 1844), p. 297.

38. Donald, 16.

39. John Taylor, 'Introduction' to *Poems Descriptive of Rural Life and Scenery* by John Clare (London: Taylor and Hessey, 1820), pp. vii-xxviii (p. x).

40. *The Textuary and Ritualist*, ed. by A Clergyman [J. W. Niblock] (London: J. Souter, 1835), pp. 142-3.

41. Ibid., p. 142.

42. Eg. 2245, fol. 306r.

43. Ibid.

44. *The Textuary and Ritualist*, pp. 143.

45. Eg. 2245, fol. 306r.

46. *Poems Descriptive*, p.11.

47. Eg. 2245, fol. 306r.

48. Ibid.

'Peasant with a Rake', Johann Christoph Erhard (German, 1795–1822), 1819, etching. The Metropolitan Museum of Art, New York.

John Clare and the Northamptonshire Dialect: Rethinking Language and Place[1]

Alex Broadhead

Which dialect did John Clare use in his poetry? I refer not to his Scots-language verse or those moments of Irish English. I am thinking, rather, of the words collected in the glossaries to his first collections, and that appear intermittently throughout his published verse; to the non-standard grammar which was occasionally pounced upon by reviewers; the same dialect, give or take a few borrowings and neologisms, that we generally assume Clare spoke and heard spoken by his neighbours. This might seem a simple question and one with a ready answer: to wit, the Northamptonshire dialect. Such is the answer given, for example, in the work of Jonathan Bate, James McKusick, Shalon Noble, Mina Gorji and Adam White.[2] And, outside academia, we find Clare's words held up as authentic examples of the Northamptonshire dialect in, for instance, a *Guardian* article by Robert MacFarlane[3] or an online gift-card shop.[4] But from a historical perspective, the question proves more complex.

In this article, I want to suggest that the idea of the Northamptonshire dialect didn't exist when Clare wrote the verse that formed his first collections. On the contrary, the Northamptonshire dialect only came into being as a consequence of successive recontextualisations of Clare's writing, years after it was first published. There is a paradox at work here, which has consequences for how we understand the (already) vexed issue of language and place in Clare's writing. In order to unpick this paradox, this article examines the role of Clare's work in the emergence of the Northamptonshire dialect. And it compares Clare's use of features now associated with Northamptonshire dialect in 'The Village Minstrel' with his use of Scots and Irish English in order to explore the implications of the preceding history for our understanding of what dialect means in Clare's writing.

Let me retrace my steps a little. What do I mean when I say that the 'idea' of the Northamptonshire dialect didn't exist when Clare was writing? To qualify that statement, some explanation of the theoretical context of this argument might be helpful. In treating a dialect not as a concrete thing, but as an idea, I am drawing on the work of the linguists Asif Agha and Barbara Johnstone. Agha has demonstrated how the idea of Received Pronunciation – a prestigious spoken form of Standard English – came to be articulated and attached to specific linguistic features in the eighteenth century before becoming disseminated, first through print, then through institutions such as public schools and latterly through mass media.[5] Following Agha, Johnstone has adapted this model for the purposes of explaining how the idea of the Pittsburghese dialect has entered public consciousness in the United States. In a 2009 article on the 'commodification' of Pittsburghese, Johnstone writes:

> Although linguistic variation is audible to someone listening for it, a dialect is not. What linguists and laypeople alike encounter in lived experience are particular speakers, writers, or signers, saying particular things in particular ways. The variation between one speaker and another, or between the same person's speech in one situation as opposed to another, is often unnoticeable to a particular hearer. In order to become noticeable, a particular variant must be linked with an ideological scheme that can be used to evaluate it in contrast to another variant.[6]

This process, by which a distinctive word or pronunciation, for instance, becomes associated with an ideological scheme, such as a place, is called enregisterment. It may seem odd, in the context of an article on John Clare, to treat a place as an ideological scheme, in light of the poet's celebrated attentiveness to the distinctive material manifestations – the flora, fauna and landmarks – of different areas. But geographical borders – on which the notion of a discrete place depends – are mutable human constructions, or 'ideological schemes', even if the humans who draw them are sometimes guided by natural boundaries such as rivers or oceans. Dialects, suggests Johnstone, are attempts to map the messy business of linguistic variation onto those human-made boundaries and borders. Those seeking an example of this mutability need look no further than Clare's native village of Helpston: in the mid-twentieth century, the redrawing of county lines resulted in the village of Helpston being reassigned from Northamptonshire, first, to the county of Huntingdon and Peterborough and, latterly, to Cambridgeshire. In one sense, Northamptonshire's most famous poet no longer comes from Northamptonshire.

The emergence of enregisterment as a means for explaining how the idea of a dialect comes into being has had an energising effect on the study of dialect writing. As Jane Hodson, Paul Cooper, Javier Ruano-Garcìa, Tony Crowley and others have shown, dialect writing, in combination with other metalinguistic commentary, both reflects and promotes the association of specific ways of talking with the idea of a place and with recognisable identity-types (the cheeky Cockney, for instance, or the dour Yorkshireman).[7] Ruano-Garcìa, for example, has shown how particular respellings in the Lancashire dialect writing of the late modern English period 'evoke shared ideas' about the distinguishing features of that dialect and how they diverge from Standard English and Received Pronunciation.[8] In so doing, Ruano-Garcìa suggests, these texts 'contribute to highlighting and enregistering that linguistic difference'.[9] Considering a more recent historical example, Crowley has drawn attention to the ways in which humorous publications such as the *Lern Yerself Scouse* series (1966-2000), along with other media, helped to establish the concepts of Scouse dialect and identity in 'the national and local imaginary'.[10]

The historical processes described by Ruano-Garcìa and Crowley are complex and multifaceted, involving what might be described as a recursive loop of writers and speakers reflecting and building on existing connections between selected linguistic features, and thereby amplifying them. Even so, the examples they discuss are relatively straightforward when contrasted with the case of Clare and his use of dialect. On the one hand, it is anachronistic to identify Clare's non-standard language with Northamptonshire dialect, insofar as Northamptonshire dialect did not exist in popular consciousness when Clare was writing. On the other hand, the idea of Northamptonshire dialect would not exist in its current form were it not for Clare's work and those, such as Thomas Sternberg and Ann Baker, who subsequently drew on it in the earliest accounts of Northamptonshire dialect.

What I seek to explain here, among other things, are some of the deeper historical reasons for the disagreement surrounding the relationship between language and place in Clare's writing. It is unnecessary, in this context, to review the great wealth of scholarship on this topic; indeed, Kövesi has explored the problematic social assumptions that occasionally encroach on representations of Clare as '*the* "poet of place," *sui generis*'. As Simon Kövesi writes:

> place has been particularly prevalent in readings of Clare because he is, like so many labouring-class poets, a writer whose situatedness – whose geographical place and socio-economic positioning – is the mainstay of the frame through which he is regarded from the outset of his poetic career.[11]

This article very much belongs to the body of work highlighted as problematic by Kövesi, insofar as place and class are two of its central concerns. Where my argument departs from existing criticism is that it attempts to theorise and historicise one of the central ideas about place and language in Clare scholarship. I seek to show that the situatedness of Clare's language is not an immanent quality of the language itself. Put another way, we should not assume that there is something irreducibly and self-evidently 'local' about words such as *crizzle, pudge* or *pooty*: those words that are so often cited as emblems of Clare's attachment to Northamptonshire dialect. As Johnstone has shown, the association of a word or any other linguistic feature with a particular locality is a historical process comprising several stages, which is not inevitable, even if it tends to follow a broadly common pattern.

Johnstone et al describe the process by which variants become linked with ideological schemes by adapting William Labov's three-part taxonomy of *indicator, marker* and *stereotype*: a framework designed to measure the extent to which speakers associate specific linguistic forms (pronunciations, for example) with a particular place or social group.[12] In place of these three terms, Johnstone et al propose (respectively): first-order, second-order and third-order indexicality. First-order indexicality refers to the geographical or social concentration of specific linguistic variables: such that using them correlates with being from a particular area or belonging to particular social categories (e.g. working-class or male). These 'correlations [may not be] noticeable' to 'socially nonmobile speakers in dense, multiplex networks'.[13] Second-order indexicality occurs when:

> speakers start to notice and attribute meaning to regional variants and shift styles in their own speech. The meaning of these forms is shaped mainly by ideologies about class and correctness, though

'Hedging and Ditching' (*Liber Studiorum*, X:47), J. M. W. Turner (1775–1851), 1812, etching. The Metropolitan Museum of Art, New York.

regional forms can also be linked with locality by people who have had the "localness" of those forms called to attention.[14]

Crucially, in these early phases – of first and second-order indexicality – dialect forms are seldom if ever used to self-consciously perform local identity, for the simple reason that their 'local' quality is only just beginning to be acknowledged. Third-order indexicality is needed for this to occur. Johnstone et al describe this phase as follows, in relation to Pittsburghese:

> People noticing the existence of second-order stylistic variation in Pittsburghers' speech link the regional variants they are most likely to hear with Pittsburgh identity, drawing on the increasingly widely circulating idea that places and dialects are essentially linked (every place has a dialect). These people [including insiders and outsiders] use regional forms drawn from highly codified lists to perform local identity, often in ironic, semiserious ways.[15]

The three phases of enregisterment, as described by Johnstone et al, map on to the history of the Northamptonshire dialect quite precisely.

In 1794, a year after the birth of John Clare, James Donaldson's *General View of the Agriculture of the County of Northampton* was published. Donaldson's report calls for the land management of the county to be overhauled, in line with the wider agricultural revolution that was happening across Britain. Its contribution to dialectology is minimal: scattered sparsely throughout the volume are a handful of local expressions, such as 'gin-balls' and 'shearlings', typically glossed as follows: 'Sixty wedders of one year old, here called Shearlings, also of the same breed, are purchased about the beginning of winter'.[16] Nevertheless, this text is the earliest listed for the county of Northamptonshire in the *Salamanca Corpus of English Dialect Writing*.[17] The Salamanca Corpus makes no claim to comprehensiveness and therefore it cannot be assumed that Donaldson's was the first publication to explicitly link regional expressions with either Northamptonshire or a named place within the county. Notwithstanding these early, fleeting references to the linguistic idiosyncrasies of Northamptonshire the first two authors to produce accounts of the dialect – Sternberg in 1851 and Baker in 1854 – both advertise the fact that they are the earliest such publications of their kind, although Sternberg is careful to acknowledge the contribution of the glossaries appended to Clare's first two volumes.[18] Additionally, John Russell Smith's 1839 *Bibliographical list of the works that have been published towards illustrating the provincial dialects of England* identifies Clare's 1821 *Poems* as the first publication to contain specimens of Northamptonshire dialect.[19]

It can be concluded, therefore, that even if extensive accounts of Northamptonshire dialect did exist before the nineteenth century, there was not a burgeoning tradition of writing on the subject of the Northamptonshire dialect. This paucity becomes especially pronounced when the entries for Northamptonshire dialect in Smith's bibliography are compared with those for Cumberland. The entry for the Cumberland dialect lists the work of eight authors and, in several cases, numerous editions or reprintings of the same pieces, suggesting that there was an appetite for such publications among local readers.[20] Thus it is, in the first decades of the nineteenth century, that while the Cumberland dialect was approaching a state of third-order indexicality, where specific forms were being repeatedly highlighted, commented upon and employed in a series of self-consciously Cumberland literary performances, the Northamptonshire dialect existed only potentially, hovering for most speakers somewhere between first and second-order indexicality, with the more mobile individuals and groups just beginning to link specific expressions with localness, but others having yet to do so.

Mobility, as Johnstone points out, is a precondition of the process by which people start to make connections between linguistic features and ideological schemes. Put another way, it is only when people begin circulating *en masse* outside their immediate communities that local ways of speaking start to become associated systematically with a specific place or a social group. It is telling, then, that Donaldson's *General View of the Agriculture of the County of Northampton* anticipates precisely such a large-scale movement when reflecting on the 'depopulation of the parish' arising from the practice of enclosing open fields, and the 'new set of people [who] must be introduced, such as hedgers, ditchers, road-makers, and labourers of every description'.[21] In 1809, the year that Clare turned sixteen, this process was already underway in the poet's native village of Helpston, as John Barrell explains:

> The Act of Parliament for the Enclosure of Helpston was passed in 1809 [...] The new public roads were staked out by the middle of 1811, the new allotments of land by the beginning of 1812, and the minor and private roads in the summer of 1813. The actual work of enclosing must have been started by 1813 at the latest, and was probably more or less completed by 1816 [...][22]

As a labourer, Clare was directly involved with the work of enclosure, being employed intermittently during these decades 'with the fencing and hedging gangs engaged on the work of enclosure',[23] even as he reflected on its devastating effect on the local ecology and community in his verse. This, along with other roles, such as serving as an apprentice gardener on the Duke of Leeds' estate and as a soldier in the Eastern Regiment of the Northampton militia, would have brought Clare into contact with people from outside his immediate community, as would the fact of migrant labourers from as far afield as Ireland passing through Helpston.[24] All of these experiences would have offered Clare and his fellow villagers multiple opportunities to pay attention to linguistic differences, thus creating the conditions for second-order indexicality, when 'speakers start to notice and attribute meaning to regional variants and shift styles in their own speech'.[25] In 1820, Clare made the first of several journeys to London, where, in Robinson's words, 'he mixed both with gentry and the varied working-class of the metropolis', resulting in further 'exposure to dialects other than Northamptonshire'.[26]

Clare was evidently sensitive to such 'regional variants': this much is apparent from the fact that he was one of the very first to commit them to print. Such sensitivity should not come as a surprise in light of his remarkable attention to the finer details of his immediate environment, as evidenced by his celebrated passages of natural description and his acutely perceptive ear, as suggested by the complex rhythms and sound structures of his poetry. That Clare sought out – and listened for – nuances of linguistic difference is plain enough from the following account of the time he spent with local gypsy communities:

> I had often heard of the mistic language and black arts which the gipseys possesd but on familiar acquantance with them I found that their mystic language was nothing then things calld by slang names like village provincialisms and that no two tribes spoke the same dilacet exactly[27]

It is notable that Clare invoked the idea of 'village provincialisms' when discussing the language of different gypsy tribes, offering as it does further evidence of the ways in which venturing outside one's own community (whether to other villages or social groups) might result in a heightened sense of its idiosyncratic linguistic features.

However, the reference to 'village provincialisms' raises a further question: namely, quite how localised was Clare's sense of his own dialect? Put another way, did Clare identify the 'provincialisms' he used primarily with the village of Helpston, or with a wider geographical schema, such as Northamptonshire or the midlands? As we have seen, when modern Clare scholars do name the dialect used by Clare, it is typically as 'Northamptonshire dialect'. An outlier can be found in the introduction to Oxford Clare, in which Eric Robinson et al make reference to the poet's 'Helpston vocabulary',[28] but do not elaborate on this. In a later article on 'John Clare's Words and Their Survival in America', Robinson shows more caution in identifying the poet's language with a single location when he observes that 'county boundaries are not language-divisions'.[29]

In contrast with those who have connected Clare's non-standard language with Northamptonshire or Helpston, the introduction to Clare's first collection, *Poems descriptive of Rural Life and Scenery* (1820), identifies his regional expressions with a much larger area:

Many of the provincial expressions, to which CLARE has been forced to have recourse, [...] form [...] part of a larger number which may be called the unwritten language of England. They were once, perhaps, as current throughout the land, and are still many of them as well-sounding and significant, as any that are sanctioned by the press. In the midland counties they are readily understood without a glossary [...] [30]

This is the only point in the collection when Clare's dialect is explicitly associated with a specific, named place. The emphasis of the introduction is placed more on the social status and education of the poet and their impact on his language than it is on geographical provenance. In part, this is attributable to the acutely status-conscious nature of early nineteenth-century literary culture, but it is also consistent with Johnstone et al's observation that 'the meaning of [second-order] forms is shaped mainly by ideologies about class and correctness'.[31] Clare's subsequent collections – published, respectively, in 1821, 1827 and 1835 – do not connect his dialect forms directly with any specific locality.

Nevertheless, the first collection sowed the seeds of the later association of Clare's language with the county of his birth, by identifying the poet on the title page as 'John Clare, a Northamptonshire peasant'. It was presumably this appellation that led Clare's early reviewers to make reference to his use of 'Northamptonshire dialect' and 'the peculiar phraseology of the Northamptonshire rustics'.[32] When Clare does acknowledge this title, as in the following passage from a letter to Allan Cunningham in 1824, it is with ambivalence. Reflecting on the class hatred infused throughout Byron's dismissive description of Robert Bloomfield in *English Bards and Scotch Reviewers* (1809), Clare imagines how he, James Hogg and Cunningham might be received by its author :

I should suppose, friend Allan, that 'The Ettrick Shepherd,' 'The Nithsdale Mason,' and 'The Northamptonshire Peasant,' are looked upon as intruders and stray cattle in the fields of the Muses (forgive the classification), and I have no doubt but our reception in that Pinfold of his lordship's 'English bards' would have been as far short of a compliment as Bloomfield's.[33]

Clare evidently takes pride in the fact that a title such as 'The Northamptonshire Peasant' binds him to writers such as Hogg and

Cunningham as part of a network of labouring-class writers. But it is also notable that Clare uses 'the Northamptonshire Peasant' in the context of describing how he, Hogg and Cunningham are viewed by social elitists such as Byron. From this perspective, the name is a brand stamped on working-class poets who, like cattle, are not suffered to stray beyond the spheres ordinarily allocated to them. Clare was only too aware of the class ideology that, as Kövesi observes, informed his public image as a 'poet of place' and here we receive a glimpse of the mixed feelings he held towards it – feelings which rather complicate the local attachments often associated with Clare, as well as the wider Romantic period.[34]

Whether he was motivated by these feelings, or others – such as his own famous dislike of borders or classification[35] – Clare did not explicitly attach his dialect forms to a specific place. But, personal motivations aside, it can be seen that the ambiguity and silence surrounding this issue in Clare's early publications coincides historically with the wider absence of representations of Helpston, Northamptonshire or midlands dialect at this time. Clare was not using dialect forms that were consistently linked in the minds of the wider readership with the idea of a particular place. As such, they did not exhibit third-order indexicality.

This would gradually begin to change as the nineteenth century progressed. As noted above, Smith's 1839 *Bibliographical list of the works that have been published towards illustrating the provincial dialects of England* presents Clare's publications as examples of Northamptonshire dialect. It is worth noting here that Smith was following the contemporary practice of dividing up dialects according to county – a practice, which as Burton and Ruthven observe, was prevalent even in spite of the 'misgivings' many nineteenth-century dialectologists held towards it.[36] Twelve years later, in 1851, Thomas Sternberg's *Dialect and Folk-Lore of Northamptonshire* was published. As noted above, Sternberg identifies the glossaries to Clare's first two collections as examples of Northamptonshire dialect. What is more, he draws on definitions from those glossaries, as in the following entries:

POOTY, *n.* A snail-shell. Clare[37]

SILE. To faint, to sink gradually.
　　"They dig the grave deeper ! your Nelly's beguil'd,
　　She said, and she *siled* on the floor."
　　　　　　　　Clare's *Poems*, 1820, p. 182 [38]

Alongside lexicographical information, Sternberg's tome describes some of the distinguishing grammatical and phonological features of Northamptonshire dialect, although he is careful not to present it as an undifferentiated and unitary entity, and comments at length on linguistic 'diversity' within the different parts of the county.[39] Sternberg also elaborates at length on the superstitions of the 'Northamptonshire peasantry'[40] and draws on the writing of Clare in citing sources for various traditions. Thus it is that Sternberg's study both makes explicit linkages between 'regional forms' and a named place, which Johnstone suggests is a necessary condition of third-order indexicality, and also helps to identify the kind of immediately recognisable 'stereotypical persona' – in this case, a superstitious, rustic, old-fashioned peasant – that third-order forms are often used to project.[41] Just as Sternberg draws on Clare's dialect forms as examples of Northamptonshire dialect, so too does he articulate a form of Northamptonshire identity that is linked with the poet's authorial persona: namely, that of the peasant poet.

Shortly after the publication of Sternberg's volume, Ann Baker's *Glossary of Northamptonshire Words and Phrases* appeared in 1854. Clare actively participated in the collation of material for Baker's *Glossary*, contributing a 'poem on the May Day festivities [...] "expressly for the present work"' and making available previously unpublished writings.[42] Bate notes that the *Glossary* comprises 'over five thousand entries, including about two thousand dialect words that had not been recorded in previous works of a similar kind'[43] and that Clare was 'credited with half of all the strictly Northamptonshire words'.[44] Evidently, by this stage, Clare was comfortable with the idea of identifying the dialect words employed in his poems with a Northamptonshire dialect. But there is simply no way of knowing whether this was the case three decades earlier, when he wrote many of the lines which would come to serve as illustrations of usage in Baker's glosses. In fact, the foregoing history suggests that it may well have not even occurred to Clare or his editors that the 'provincialisms' of his writing belonged to a unitary Northamptonshire dialect (as opposed to, say, a midlands or a Helpston dialect). What can be said with certainty is that by the mid-1850s, the Northamptonshire dialect now existed as an idea with a place-based name and an accompanying list of linguistic forms attached to it. Here, then, is evidence of the final stage of enregisterment: namely, third-order indexicality. In the 1820s, this had not been the case.

'The Farm-Yard with the Cock' (*Liber Studiorum*, IV:17),
J. M. W. Turner (1775–1851), 1809, etching and mezzotint.
The Metropolitan Museum of Art, New York.

Notwithstanding the sudden conspicuousness of
Northamptonshire dialect in print, several of the characteristics
that Johnstone attributes to third-order indexicality had yet to
manifest themselves. Johnstone observes how, in twentieth-
century Pittsburgh, a small 'subset of features' from a 'highly
codified repertoire' became used in 'reflexive performances of local
identities'.[45] In other words, a handful of stereotypical linguistic
features could be used to invoke a Pittsburghese dialect and identity.
In print, at least, a comparable development does not appear to have
happened in the wake of Sternberg's and Baker's dictionaries, or
indeed Wright's *English Dialect Dictionary* (1898-1905), which
employed quotations from Clare's work to gloss words identified as
belonging to the Northamptonshire dialect.[46] As far as I have been
able to ascertain, no tradition of Northamptonshire dialect writing
emerged in the second half of the nineteenth century and there was
no well-known Northamptonshire equivalent to the stage Cockney
or Yorkshireman. The faint sparks of a 'highly codified repertoire'
of Northamptonshire dialect terms appeared around the time of
the second world war, and after, in the form of the Rushden-born

writer Reginald Norman, or R. W. N., whose dialect poems and *Air Ada* comic strip series, produced in collaboration with Peter Nevitt, were published in the *Northamptonshire Evening Telegraph* in the 1950s[47] and helped to keep the idea of a Northamptonshire vernacular alive in print. The strips would be invoked several decades after their original appearance in Butler and Eaton's *Learn Yersalf Northamptonshire Dialect* (1998). This publication was evidently modelled, as many other books of the last few decades have been, on Fritz Spiegl's popular *Lern Yerself Scouse* series of the 1960s.[48] Butler and Eaton's volume contains information, not just about the lexis and pronunciation of the Northamptonshire dialect, but also, like Sternberg's 1851 volume, local lore and history. Tellingly, *Learn Yersalf Northamptonshire Dialect* also devotes a sub-section to John Clare: the only individual to whom this honour is given in the book. Here not only the work of Clare but the person himself is recruited as an iconic figure in order to substantiate the idea of a Northamptonshire dialect, much as the more general stereotypical figure of the superstitious peasant was invoked by Sternberg in the nineteenth century.

In the present day, Clare's name remains bound up with the Northamptonshire dialect. And in a number of those instances where the two are linked, we see the emergence of something resembling a codified list of local terms: *crizzle, pooty* and *pudge* being chief among the words cited. Some of the contexts in which this occurs are, as might be expected, literary, such as a *Guardian* article by Robert Macfarlane, advertising his ecologically-conscious dialect glossary,[49] *Landmarks*, or a Twitter post publicising an episode of the BBC Radio 4 programme, *In Our Time*, which focuses on Clare.[50] *Crizzle* appears both in Macfarlane's article and in the Twitter post, where it also appears alongside *pooty, crump, gulsh, prog,* and *clock o' clay. Crizzling* appears again in a post on Michael Quinion's language-themed website, *World Wide Words*, in which it is connected to Clare and the Northamptonshire dialect (via Macfarlane's *Landmarks*).[51] Perhaps most revealingly, a number of words, including *crizzle, pooty, lady-cow* and *throstle*, have appeared on gift cards that celebrate Northamptonshire dialect and John Clare and are advertised online.[52] Here may be viewed something resembling the kind of 'dialect commodification' observed in Pittsburgh by Johnstone, where the proliferation of T-shirts, mugs and other 'material artifacts' bearing dialect words and other emblems of regional identity help to 'standardize local speech' and connect it with 'particular social meanings'.[53] Of course, one set of gift cards hardly constitutes an industry, or even a market trend. Nevertheless, that an artist has chosen to explore the commercial possibilities of these words as Northamptonshire dialect suggests (along with the other examples) the existence of a limited number of third-order forms closely linked to the idea of John Clare as a local icon.

How widespread and how enduring these linkages will prove to be is difficult to say. It is not clear, for instance, whether the salience of *crizzle* as a feature of Northamptonshire dialect is particularly pronounced for speakers living in the region, or whether it is only salient in more niche and predominantly written contexts, such as those discussed above. Regardless, it has been shown that Clare's work, in which local linguistic features are employed and – more importantly – flagged up as meaningful in prefaces and glossaries, helped to create the conditions for the kind of third-order indexicality represented by Baker's, Sternberg's and Butler and Eaton's accounts of the Northamptonshire dialect, as well as the more recent examples.

It is evident that the identification of Clare's non-standard features with Northamptonshire dialect was a retroactive process, imposed after the event. What seems to have occurred over the last two hundred years is a phenomenon described by Coupland in a 2009 article on 'mediated vernaculars'. Coupland's work in this area focuses predominantly on mass media in the late modern period, investigating how 'vernacular styles and performances find their meaning in different contexts of mediation',[54] such as social media and television advertisements. He writes:

> Late modernity tends to disembed voices from the social matrices we have taken to be primary (e.g., [...] class and regional designations [...]) and infuse new meanings into them as they are recontextualized.[55]

Where, traditionally, sociolinguistics has tended to assume that linguistic variables unproblematically index the social and regional background of speakers, the rise of broadcast and online media has required that analysts attend to the ways in which dialect can become unmoored from these fixed categories through acts of recontextualisation. Much of the subsequent work on the relationship between media and 'sociolinguistic change' has focused, as might be expected, on television, radio and the internet.[56] But it can be seen that the print media of earlier centuries behaved in comparable ways: the recontextualisation of Clare's writing in different editions, in review articles and in dialect dictionaries served to infuse a new identity into the dialect expressions he employed. What makes the case of Clare different from the examples discussed by Coupland, however, is that it is through the act of recontextualisation that the 'class and regional designations' of his language have come to be defined and reinforced. Thus the textual history of Clare's work reveals *not* that his dialect has become disembedded from a particular place, in the manner described by Coupland, but rather that it has come to be infused with a specific regional identity (Northamptonshire dialect) as a result of successive recontextualisations. Clare's work did not, by itself, enregister the Northamptonshire dialect; rather, the mediation of Clare's work by other writers brought about the enregisterment of the Northamptonshire dialect, with the result that his dialect expressions are now read retroactively, anachronistically even, as examples of that linguistic variety.

All this, of course, raises the question of precisely how we should read Clare's use of dialect forms in his poetry. What do they index, if not the regional identity of the writer and his writing? In a forthcoming article on Clare's early experiments in dialect writing, such as 'Love Epistles between Richard and Kate' and 'Lobin Clouts Satirical Sollilouquy on the Times', I explore this question in more depth.[57] It is clear in these early poems, with their dense and startling use of macrons and apostrophes, that, from very early on in his writing career, Clare was interested in the stylistic and formal possibilities of dialect representation.

Beyond these poems, however, what is striking about so many of the moments when Clare employs his own dialect (or something close to it) is the absence of those cues that, as Coupland puts it in a 2007 monograph, help to 'styl[e] a meaningful sense of place, or indeed places (plural) in meaningful contrast to each other'.[58] Framing the dialect within reported speech, including an explicit metalinguistic comment, drawing on stereotypical or recognisably 'local' personae or emblems, switching definitively from one variety to another: these are moves that a writer might make in order to 'style a meaningful sense of place'. And, indeed, we find Clare using precisely these devices in his Scots songs: whether through first lines such as 'Farewell! Auld Scotland, hills, and moors'[59] or titles such as 'Roll thee in my Tartan plaidie',[60] or through the adoption of stereotypical masks and stances, such as the exile 'turn'd out o' doors' (l.3) in the former poem. Likewise, in '[Och by jasus hes a irish lad]', it is clear that Clare is styling an Irish English voice, both from the first line and the evocation of stereotypical ideas about Irish drinking in such lines as 'By jasus judy fill the bowl / While whiskeys to be had' (ll. 5-6).[61] Coupland suggests that 'principal language zone[s]' such as Ireland and Scotland have 'familiar metalinguistic discourses of accent and dialect variation focused on sociolinguistic stereotypes', and therefore lend themselves to the performance of place.[62] And it is precisely because the nominally Northamptonshire dialect forms used by Clare did not belong to 'familiar metalinguistic discourses', that they did not possess the same potential to style a meaningful sense of place.

The absence of comparable acts of framing in many of the instances when Clare employs what we now think of as Northamptonshire dialect is perhaps what has given rise to so much of the debate surrounding his language, not least the 'editing wars' described by Kövesi.[63] It may also have prompted Hodson to observe that 'it is simply not possible to determine exactly which features of his non-standard language Clare intended to achieve a "deliberate effect"'.[64] Hodson goes on to comment that 'from a reader's perspective the perception of intentionality can matter a great deal'[65] and, indeed, the case of Clare reveals that, in the absence of such cues, readers (or at least literary scholars) will project meaning on to the language.

One rare but instructive example of Clare explicitly framing language now associated with Northamptonshire dialect can be found in 'The Village Minstrel' (1821). In the following passage, women try to persuade their husbands and beaus to buy a wreath or ribbon from a market stall. Clare makes use of <yah> a non-standard spelling of you. It is telling that the entry for 'yah' which appears in Anne Baker's *Glossary of Northamptonshire Words and Phrases* cites this very passage as its source.[66] Clare writes:

> Where cakes & nuts & ginger bread & all
> Tempt clowns to buy & far more tempting still
> Where shining ribbons dizen out the stall
> & wenches drag poor sheepish bob or bill
> Some long dallied promise to fulfill
> New wreath or bow for sunday cap to buy
> 'If yah set any store by one yah will'
> Each strings his purse & makes me no reply
> But thinks returns at night will suit for clowns are smuttly sly
> (ll. 690-8)

This, the manuscript version of the poem, is a little confusing insofar as it is not clear who 'me' refers to in the second-to-last line ('me' was altered to 'them' in the published version[67]). Regardless, it is evident that Clare is drawing on a misogynistic stereotype in this passage: that of the 'henpecking' working-class wife, a common trope in non-standard writing, which we find, for instance, in the form of Tam's angry wife in Burns's 'Tam o' Shanter, a tale' (1793), or 'The Cumberland Scold' by Susanne Blamire and Catherine Gilpin (1842).[68] Three elements work to frame 'yah' as a marker of this identity: firstly, the use of direct speech presentation; secondly, the physicality of the scene (specifically, the fact that the women 'drag' their partners), and thirdly, the fact that their partners are identified as 'clowns'. 'Yah' is put into the mouth of a character (or characters) described by the narrator in socially meaningful ways. The gender and the class of the speaker is what the dialect indexes in this passage, and not her regional identity, even if 'yah' is a form drawn from Clare's immediate locality.

In contrast, consider the less conspicuous use of another dialect feature in the passage: namely, the verb 'dizen', which Baker glosses as 'to dress out, more particularly in holiday finery'.[69] There is little in the way of framing here: no direct speech and no attempt within the passage or the poem itself to identify it with a particular social identity. When, across his work, Clare employs linguistic features which have subsequently come to be identified as Northamptonshire dialect, this pattern of *not* employing cues to associate linguistic features with a specific social identity is by far the most common. Of course, a reader may choose to project social meaning on to the word 'dizen', for instance by reading it as a marker of Clare's regional identity or educational status, but this will most probably be influenced by knowledge of the author's background gleaned from separate texts or paratexts: in short, by a context in which Clare's work has been mediated. To say this is not to argue that Clare was not in control of the meaning of his work: rather, that in this instance as in many others, he has not chosen to foreground the social (as opposed to the denotative) meaning of a dialect feature.

Clare's responses to Taylor's suggestions for corrections when editing 'The Village Minstrel' help to illuminate in miniature the disparities that might exist between the way that writers and their readers perceive the same non-standard expressions. Taylor in one letter commented that –

We have but few Provincialisms in the poem, & I should be glad if we could get rid of One that is left *himsen*; but if it cannot be easily done never mind.– Real English Country words are different in my mind & should be judged differently from those which are only peculiar to a district, & perhaps *himsen* & *shanny* are of the latter class. – Shanny is not used beyond the Trent, tho' himsen is common enough I know.[70]

Here Taylor distinguishes between an idealised national pastoral, or 'Country', vocabulary on the one hand and regional dialect on the other. He has in mind, we might infer, something close to the synthetic diction of the Spenserian pastoral mode, comprised of archaisms and expressions from different dialects, which according to Mina Gorji, held a strong appeal for Clare.[71] The extant evidence of Clare's letters indicate that he did not reply directly to Taylor's comments concerning *himsen* and *shanny*. This apparent silence – whatever the reason for it – is consistent at least with his more general unwillingness to enter into a finely-grained discussion of the provenance of individual words. His first reply to Taylor focuses predominantly on his editor's reservations about the name of the poem, but in a subsequent letter, Clare briefly comments that 'all provincialisms & every thing else requird shall be readily answerd when wishd'.[72] Regardless, the two words were retained in the published version of the poem.

Commenting on Taylor's objection to these words, Edward Storey suggests that the editor misunderstood Clare's motivations, insofar as 'It is the Northamptonshire flavour of his dialect words which is important to him, something distinctive and particularised'.[73] In fact, Clare's later commentary on 'The Village Minstrel' suggest that his sense of the geographical identity of the poem was both more specific than Taylor would have liked and less fixed than Storey proposes. In an autobiographical fragment, Clare notes that he 'began the Village Minstrel a long while before attempting to describe my own feelings and love for rural objects.' He goes on to reveal how he came to dislike it for the reason that 'it does not describe the feelings of a ryhming peasant strongly or localy enough'.[74] We have seen, in his letter to Allan Cunningham, that Clare's attitude towards the geographical labelling of labouring-class poets was complex and two-sided. Here it is apparent that these feelings deepened and changed over time. Clare in his autobiographical writings testifies to a dawning awareness of the ways in which place, class and feeling intersect – a shift in perspective which caused him to look back on his earlier writings with a different eye. What is missing in these comments, however, is a fourth element: language, and that, I would like to suggest, is because the dialect spoken by Clare had yet to coalesce around a single idea of a place.

There is, it may be argued, a danger of historical determinism in arguing that Clare could not write in Northamptonshire dialect or perform Northamptonshire identity because it did not exist at the time. Could he not, we might ask, have invented Northamptonshire dialect and used it consciously and performatively, for instance by naming his collection *Poems in the Northamptonshire dialect*? To which the answer is: yes, he hypothetically could have, but he did not. And perhaps one of the aspects of his use of dialect that makes it so unusual and compelling is that Clare was not anxious to give it a name or circumscribe it geographically. It might also be argued that in offering an historical explanation for Clare's linguistic practice, we undervalue both his own creativity and idiosyncrasy and, likewise, the nuanced stylistic effects set in motion by his language. In a forthcoming article I discuss some of these effects in more detail and how they might be squared with the history sketched thus far. Clare's early experiments in dialect writing, I suggest, use language not to style place, but to explore the complex ways in which class, self-perception and interpersonal relationships intersect.[75]

We do Clare a disservice if we imagine him simply drawing on the resources of a readily-available, easily-identifiable and well-defined regional dialect. To do so is not only to overlook the role of his work in the invention of the idea of that dialect, but also to overlook the nature of the meanings that arise from linguistic variation in his early dialect writing. But the implications of this stretch far beyond a handful of minor, unpublished poems. Rather, they call for a wholesale reconsideration of how we approach the relationship between language and place in Clare's entire oeuvre.

NOTES

1   The author wishes to express gratitude for the very useful comments of the anonymous referee who reviewed this article.
2   Bate, *Biography*, p. 463; James McKusick, 'John Clare and the Tyranny of Grammar', *Studies in Romanticism*, 33.2 (1994), 255-77 (p. 257); Shalon Noble, '"Homeless at Home": John Clare's Uncommon Ecology', *Romanticism*, 21.2 (2015), 171-81 (174); Mina Gorji, *John Clare and the Place of Poetry* (Liverpool: Liverpool University Press, 2008), p. 74; Adam White, *John Clare's Romanticism* (Cham: Palgrave Macmillan, 2017), p. 288.

3   Robert Macfarlane, 'The word-hoard: Robert Macfarlane on rewilding our language of landscape', *Guardian*, 27 February 2015 <https://www.theguardian.com/books/2015/feb/27/robert-macfarlane-word-hoard-rewilding-landscape> [accessed 3 March 2021].

4   'Jamie Poole' <https://www.downtoearthcards.co.uk/artist-cards-grouped-by-artist/jamie-poole.html?p=2> [accessed 3 March 2021].

5   Asif Agha, 'The social life of cultural value', *Language and Communication*, 23 (2003), 231-73.

6   Barbara Johnstone, 'Pittsburghese Shirts: Commodification and the Enregisterment of an Urban Dialect', *American Speech*, 84.2 (2009), 115-45 (p. 159-60).

7   Jane Hodson, *Dialect in British Fiction* (Basingstoke: Palgrave Macmillan, 2014), pp. 74-5; Paul Cooper, '"Deregisterment" and "fossil forms": the cases of gan and mun in "Yorkshire" dialect', *English Today*, 33.1 (2017), 43-52; Javier Ruano-Garcìa, J., 'He towd her soe monny a mad farrant Tele: On flotsam, respellings and the enregisterment of l-vocalisation and /a/+nasal in the Late Modern Lancashire dialect', *Altre Modernità*, (2020), 16-34; Tony Crowley, *Scouse: A Cultural and Social History* (Liverpool: Liverpool University Press, 2012), pp .99-105.

8   Ruano Garcìa, (p. 17).

9   Ruano Garcìa, (p. 17).

10   Crowley, p. 110.

11   Simon Kövesi, *John Clare: Nature, Criticism and History* (London: Palgrave Macmillan, 2017), pp. 1-2.

12   Johnstone, Barbara, Jennifer Andrus and Andrew E. Danielson, 'Mobility, Indexicality, and the Enregisterment of "Pittsburghese"', *Journal of English Linguistics*, 34.2 (2006), 77-104.

13   Johnstone et al. (p. 82).

14   Johnstone et al (p. 82).

15   Johnstone et al (p. 83).

16   James Donaldson, *General View of the Agriculture of the County of Northampton* (Edinburgh: printed by Adam Neill and Company, 1794), p. 25, p. 51.

17   Lidia Alonso Rodríguez and María F. García-Bermejo Giner, 'James Donaldson', *The Salamanca Corpus: Digital Archive of English Dialect Texts* <http://www.thesalamancacorpus.com/varia_em_nthp_1700-1799_donaldson_general_1794.html> [accessed: 3 March 2021]

18   Ann Baker, *Glossary of Northamptonshire Words and Phrases* (London: John Russell Smith, 1854), p. xi; Thomas Sternberg, *The Dialect and Folk-Lore of Northamptonshire* (London: John Russell Smith, 1851), p. iii.

19   John Russell Smith, *A Bibliographical List of the Works that have been Published, Towards Illustrating the Principal Dialects of England*, (London: John Russell Smith, 1839), p. 15.

20   See Smith, p. 5-8.

21   Donaldson, p. 60.

22   John Barrell, *The Idea of Landscape and the Sense of Place* (Cambridge: Cambridge University Press, 1972), p. 106.

23   Bate, p. 80.

24   Bate, p. 71, 77 and 52.

25   Johnstone et al (p. 82).

26   Eric Robinson, 'John Clare's Words and Their Survival in America', *Wordsworth Circle*, 41.2 (2010), 94-8 (p. 95).

27   John Clare, '[Gipseys]' in *By Himself*, pp. 83-7, p. 83.

28   *Early Poems*, I, pp. ix-xxiv, p. xii.

29   Robinson, 'John Clare's Words', p. 94.

30   'Introduction', *Poems Descriptive of Rural Life and Scenery* (London: Taylor and Hessey, 1820), pp. vii-xxviii, p. xvi.

31   Johnstone et al (p. 82).

32   From an unsigned review, *Monthly Magazine*, November 1821, pp. 321-5 (repr. in *Critical Heritage*, pp. 150-6, p. 154).

33   To Allan Cunningham, 9 September 1824, *Letters*, pp. 302-3.

34   See for instance Fiona Stafford, *Local Attachments: The Province of Poetry* (Oxford: Oxford University Press, 2010), p. 20.

35   See for instance Eric Miller, 'Enclosure and Taxonomy in John Clare', *Studies in English Literature*, 40.4 (2000), 635-57.

36   T. L. Burton and K. K. Ruthven, 'General Introduction', in *The Complete Poems of William Barnes*, Vol. I: *Poems in the Broad Form of the Dorset Dialect*, ed. by T. L. Burton and K. K. Ruthven (Oxford: Oxford University Press, 2013), pp. xxi-cxii, p. liv.

37   Sternberg, p. 83.

38   Sternberg, p. 94.

39   Sternberg, p. ix.

40   Sternberg, p. 132.

41   Johnstone (p. 160).

42   Bate, *Biography*, p. 514.

43   Ibid.

44   Ibid.

45   Johnstone et al (p. 84).

46   See for instance the entry for 'crizzle' in Joseph Wright, *The English Dialect Dictionary*, 6 vols (Oxford: Oxford University Press, 1898-1905), I, p. 799.

47   Mia Butler and Colin Eaton, *Learn Yersalf Northamptonshire Dialect* (Dereham: Nostalgia Publications, 1998), p. 34.

48   See for instance Frank Shaw, Fritz Spiegl and Stan Kelley, *Lern Yerself Scouse: How to Talk Proper in Liverpool* (Liverpool: Scouse Press, 1966).

49   Robert Macfarlane, 'The word-hoard: Robert Macfarlane on rewilding our language of landscape', *Guardian*, 27 February 2015 <https://www.theguardian.com/books/2015/feb/27/robert-macfarlane-word-hoard-rewilding-landscape> [accessed 3 March 2021].

50   BBC *In Our Time* Twitter feed, 11 February 2017: 'John Clare: bringing pooty back. And crizzle, crump, gulsh, prog, clock-o'-clay...' <https://twitter.com/BBCInOurTime/status/830335298546581504?s=20> [accessed 17 June 2020].

51   Michael Quinion, 'Crizzling' <http://www.worldwidewords.org/weirdwords/ww-cr15.htm> [accessed 3 March 2021].

52   'Jamie Poole', *Down to Earth Cards* <https://www.downtoearthcards.co.uk/artist-cards-grouped-by-artist/jamie-poole.html?p=2> [accessed 3 March 2021].

53   Johnstone, (p. 157).

54   Coupland, Nikolas, 'The Mediated Performance of Vernaculars', *Journal of English Linguistics*, 37.3 (2009), 284-300 (p. 288).

55   Coupland, 'Mediated Performance of Vernaculars' (p. 298).

56   See for instance the essays collected in *Mediatization and Sociolinguistic Change*, ed. by Jannis Androutsopoulos (Berlin: De Gruyter, 2014).

57   See Alex Broadhead, 'John Clare's early experiments in dialect writing', forthcoming.

58   Nikolas Coupland, *Style: Language Variation and Identity* (Cambridge: Cambridge University Press, 2007), p. 121.

59   *Later Poems*, I, p. 290.

60   *Later Poems*, II, p. 1083-4.

61   John Clare, *A Champion for the Poor: Political Verse and Prose*, ed. by P. M. S. Dawson, Eric Robinson and David Powell (Ashington: Carcanet, 2000), p. 159-60.

62   Coupland, *Style*, p. 123.

63   Kövesi, pp. 127-40.

64   Jane Hodson, 'Literary Uses of Dialect', in *The Oxford Handbook of British Romanticism*, ed. by David Duff (Oxford: Oxford University Press, 2018), pp. 513-28, p. 522-3.

65   Hodson, p. 523.

66   See Baker, p. 410, which directs the reader to the entry for 'store', p. 301, in which 'yah' is exemplified by this passage from 'The Village Minstrel'.

67   John Clare, *The Village Minstrel* (London: Taylor and Hessey, 1821), p. 34.

68   See lines 17-32 of Robert Burns, 'Tam o' Shanter', in *The Poems and Songs of Robert Burns*, ed. by James Kinsley, 3 vols (Oxford: Oxford University Press, 1968), III, pp. 557-64; Catherine Gilpin and Susanne Blamire, 'The Cumberland Scold', in *The Poetical Works of Miss Susanna Blamire* (Edinburgh: John Menzies 1842), pp. 211-13, in *Eighteenth-Century Poetry Archive* <https://www.eighteenthcenturypoetry.org/works/bsb18-w0580.shtml> [accessed: 5 July 2019].

69   Baker, p. 187.

70   From John Taylor to John Clare, 23 January 1821, *Letters*, pp. 144-5, p. 145.

71   Mina Gorji, *John Clare and the Place of Poetry* (Liverpool: Liverpool University Press, 2008), pp. 77-96.

72   To John Taylor, 13 February 1821, *Letters*, pp. 150-2, p. 152.

73   Edward Storey, *The Poetry of John Clare: A Critical Introduction* (London: Routledge, 1973), p. 95.

74   *By Himself*, pp. 34-116, p. 113-4.

75   Broadhead, 'John Clare's early experiments in dialect writing'

'Come prime your Guns': Fellowship, protest and performance in John Clare's Robin Hood ballads and 'The Poachers'

Stephen Ridgwell

Poachers, like smugglers, enjoyed considerable sympathy in their localities. They retained something of the Robin Hood spirit
                                        Christopher Hill, 1997

Why should you not give us an improved Robin Hood?
                            John Taylor to Clare, 20 May 1826[1]

Between Clare's first meeting with John Taylor in 1819 and his admission to the Northampton General Lunatic Asylum in 1841, the Robin Hood legend saw a remarkable resurgence. As the largely agrarian society into which Clare was born gave way to an urban-industrial one, tales of greenwood carnivalesque appealed to a broad constituency of writers and readers. Ranging from the high Toryism of Walter Scott to the more liberally-minded poets of the Cockney School, and on through the nameless consumers of penny broadsides and Robin Hood garlands, as fact-based legend or deeply ingrained folk-myth this medieval poacher of the king's deer had a far-reaching appeal. Full of manly deeds, sometimes subversive, and steeped in good fellowship, the tales spoke powerfully to Clare. A youthful reader of the garlands, and later of Joseph Ritson's *All the Ancient Poems, Songs, and Ballads, Now Extant, Relative to that Celebrated English Outlaw* (first published in 1795), in the fertile interlude between *The Village Minstrel* and *The Shepherd's Calendar* Clare combined an active interest in song collection with imitation of the 'old poets' to produce his own pair of Robin Hood-themed ballads.

First noticed in the 1960s by Margaret Grainger, and published for the first time in George Deacon's 1983 study of Clare and the folk tradition, they have also figured in Mina Gorji's work on literary sociability and the idea of Merry England.[2] Deacon also included the poet's version of 'Robin Hood and the Three Squires' which, while not original to Clare, shows his rich knowledge of the source material. In its best-known form, this seventeenth-century broadside includes the rescue of three men sentenced to hang for poaching, and Clare certainly had access to this text via print, but might have known it orally too. What none of the existing scholarship has done, however, is to link these Helpston Robin Hoods – especially Clare's 'Robin Hood & the Gamekeepers' – to another piece unpublished in his lifetime, but found in his guardbook (Pet. MS A40), the middle-period poem 'The Poachers'.[3] Although here we should mention *Champion for the Poor*, an edited collection of Clare's more obviously political prose and verse which not only includes 'Robin Hood & the Gamekeepers', and 'How they robbed the priest of Lorn' (basically a drinking song set in 'old merry sherwood'), but also 'The Poachers'[4]. Bearing some resemblance to 'The Gipseys Song' (1825) in its celebration of lawlessness and allusion to 'The Lincolnshire Poacher' ('Bad luck to tyrant majistrates [...] success to gipseys all'), the poem frames the illegal taking of game as part of a wider struggle against the forces of tyranny.[5]

An essential word in the oppositional lexicon of the period, and one often used by Clare, 'tyranny' was readily employed by critics to explain and condemn the 'curst improvement' of parliamentary enclosure.[6] While the effects of this process continue to be debated, and there were gains as well as losses, between *c.* 1760 and 1820 its impact was especially felt in open-field counties like Northamptonshire where the hedges and fences that labourers like Clare helped to erect meant the rights of the propertied being visibly re-stated as paramount. In words deplored as 'radical slang' by his self-appointed moral guide Lord Radstock, Clare wrote 'Each tyrant fixt his sign [...] To hint a trespass now who crossd the ground'.[7] At the same time of course, these legal and physical markers of exclusion provided extra excitement for the galloping riders of the Milton enthusiastically described by Clare just after Helpston's own enclosure had been completed: 'The cracking whip & scarlet coat [...] The hardiest hunter wins'.[8] Aside from enhancing the sport of one of the country's leading fox-hunts, and affording Clare the chance to flatter a patron, this reshaping of the landscape did much to facilitate the enclosure of game into carefully managed preserves, a development also linked to improvements in firearms and the attendant demand of 'hardnd gunners' for more birds to shoot at.[9]

Now mostly associated with a peaceful and settled countryside, in the opening decades of the nineteenth century these privileged recreational spaces were witness to serious violence between well-armed poaching gangs and those employed to stop them.[10] Crucial to this conflict was the commonly held belief that whatever its motivation – hunger, profit, protest, sport – to take animals deemed to be wild was not to commit a crime in the usual sense. As Thomas Bewick observed, 'to convince the intelligent poor man, that the fowls of the air were created only for the rich, is impossible and will forever remain so'.[11] But if scripture said that nature's bounty was granted to all, a mass of statutes and legal manuals consistently declared otherwise, to say nothing of stern public moralists such as George Crabbe who worried how 'The poacher questions, with perverted mind, / were not the gifts of heaven for all designed?'[12] Disdained by Clare for writing like a magistrate, along with reforming MPs like Sir Samuel Romilly the author of 'Smugglers and Poachers' (1819) was equally troubled by the laws protecting the interests of game preservers. 'Enough, my lord, do hares and pheasants cost', was a line of Crabbe's that could easily have been one of Clare's.[13]

By no means an innovation, the earliest game law dates from 1389 (overlaying even earlier Norman forest laws); in tandem with the accelerated drive to enclose, these laws not only came to be more comprehensive, but also – ostensibly at least – they were more comprehensively enforced. In Northamptonshire, for example, an Association for the Preservation of Game was instituted in 1800, while the *Stamford Mercury* regularly carried notices against trespassers and poachers issued by prominent sporting landowners like the Fitzwilliams and the Exeters.[14] Implicit in both 'The Poachers' and 'The Gipseys Song' is what in *Liberty Against the Law* Christopher Hill termed the 'Robin Hood spirit'.[15] Suggestively for us, Hill's book not only includes a pair of chapters on the famous outlaw, but also considerations of poaching, gypsies, and Clare himself. Taking this notion of the Robin Hood spirit, and the ways it might be related to mid-1820s Clare, I want to consider how he used poems like 'The Poachers' and 'Robin Hood & the Gamekeepers' not only to explore themes of good fellowship and legitimate protest, but also to stage a kind of wood-bound personal performance.

Whatever the slipperiness of his politics, Clare's excursion into poaching displays a distinctly radical edge and marks another front in his literary war against the forces of enclosure. If poaching has proved a useful 'weapon of the weak', or in more figurative terms an everyday 'tactic' for the disempowered, it was one well-suited to Clare, especially when played out in the densely symbolic environs of the wood.[16] Writing within what Bridget Keegan discerns as the 'long literary tradition within which trees and forests had been used for symbolic explorations of political rights and responsibilities', these poems attest to what might be viewed as Clare's situated connectedness.[17] The poacher's 'muttering gun' and stories of Robin Hood were woven into Clare's Helpston life, but as well as the local and the personal there was also the general and the national.[18] With the contentious workings of the game laws generating a blizzard of pamphlets, articles and reform bills, and with interest in the outlaw legend burgeoning, they also formed part of a wider debate. At a peak moment of creativity, it was one which the 'trespasser' poet, the 'outlaw' poet, or as Roger Sales has it the 'poacher-poet', was fully joined to.[19]

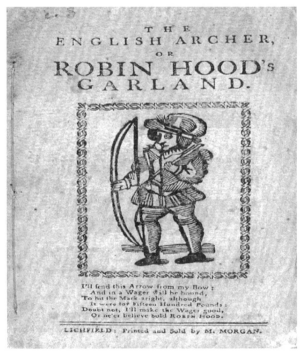

A typical Robin Hood's garland from Staffordshire (c. 1780), closely modelled on the Dicey garland.

'the merriest set of fellows I ever met with': Sociability and Fellowship

In Book V of *The Prelude* Wordsworth fondly recalled the popular stories of his youth: 'Of Jack the giant-killer, Robin Hood, / And Sabra in the forest with St. George! / The child, whose love is here, at least, / doth reap one precious gain, that he forgets himself'.[20] To this might be compared Clare's own remembering: 'The first books I got hold of beside the bible and prayer book was an old book of Essays with no title and then a large one on Farming [and] Robin hood's Garland and the Scotch Rogue'.[21] Before *Robinson Crusoe*, which Clare also came to know early in life, and before his seminal encounter with James Thomson's *The Seasons*, the stories of Robin Hood formed some of the first writing Clare became familiar with, as indeed was the case for Wordsworth and a great many others. Most commonly such texts were gathered in cheaply printed garlands like that first produced by the London and Northampton-based firm of Dicey in *c*. 1760. Trading through well-established distribution networks, and offering all manner of chapbooks, broadsides and elementary primers, such publishing enterprises were crucial in bringing education and entertainment to places like Helpston.

For attentive readers like Clare, the cultural work performed by the Dicey garland, or the numerous others like it, was not just confined to the ballads. Along with the accompanying woodcut images, there would also be a preface in which some basic historical details were given – the assumption being that Robin Hood and his men had actually lived, though dates and locations could vary. The central 'fact' contained in such accounts – and which through the ancient play-games and festivals attaching to his name had long passed into the vernacular – was that he exemplified good fellowship and was a friend to the poor and the weak. Or as the prospectus-like title of another popular garland had it, *The Exploits of the Renowned Robin Hood; The Terror of Forestallers and Engrossers, and the Protector of the Poor and Helpless*. The continuing resonance of these tales and ballads into adulthood, as well as their moral acceptability, is captured in Clare's loving description of a woodman's Sunday evening 'humming oer an anthem hymn or psalm / Nor does he think a ballad any harm / But often carrols oer his cottage hearth / "Bold robin hood" the "Shipwreck" or the "storm"'.[22]

The livingness of these stories is also evident in 'The Village Minstrel', a work in which the newly-minted poet embraces his cultural roots and finds his alter-ego Lubin 'enrapturd' by herdsmen singing 'Bout feats of robin hood & little john / Whose might was feard by country & by king'.[23] At the heart of this appreciation of the outlaw was that contrary to the disguised aristocrat reported by Jonathan Bate this evergreen hero was traditionally cast as a yeoman.[24] Ultimately loyal to the crown, if not necessarily its representatives, any services rendered flowed from the free-born choice of the commoner rather than noble obligation. Looking to Clare's attempts at writing the outlaw, and his closely-paired representation in 'The Poachers', it should be stressed that the Robin Hoods Clare first knew, and which formed his template, almost entirely lacked a female element. The outlaw always had company at his forest table, but it was never Maid Marian's. Anticipating, and perhaps reflecting, Clare's time with *London Magazine*'s 'merriest set of fellows I ever met with', this was a distinctly homosocial world of brotherly liberty.[25] Given the extensive black market then operating, it is not altogether fanciful to see this Jack i' the Green (or indeed Percy Green) enjoying lively Fleet Street dinners of poached game with 'lads of rare promise' such as J. H. Reynolds, Charles Lamb and T. G. Wainewright.[26]

At around the time he was writing 'The Village Minstrel', Clare was rediscovering many of the songs and stories of his youth through Thomas Percy's *Reliques of Ancient Poetry*. A work that by his own admission 'redeemed' Wordsworth, this influential collection of *Old Heroic Ballads, Songs and Other Pieces of our Earlier Poets* first appeared in 1765 and by 1812 had run to a fifth edition.[27] Introduced to it in the summer of 1820, Clare not only found in the *Reliques* 'all the stories of my grandmother & her gossiping neighbours' but also a ballad he couldn't previously have known – the intense and unusually violent 'Robin Hood and Guy of Gisborne'.[28] He would also have discovered 'Adam Bell, Clim of the Clough, and William of Cloudesly', a stirring sixteenth-century tale of three north-country yeoman outlawed for poaching deer and now sworn to stand as brothers-in-arms. However, if the garlands and Percy, along with the oral tradition, had given Clare the bulk of the Robin Hood canon, it was acquiring Ritson's work in 1824 that finally completed his collection. And whether he needed it or not, thanks to the Jacobin-supporting Ritson's ideologically charged introduction (for example, the 'barbarous' Norman forest laws are clearly made analogous to the current system of game laws), Clare had ringing confirmation of the outlaw's determined opposition to 'complicated tyranny' and his populist spirit of 'freedom and independence'.[29] As Clare would put it in 'Robin & The Gamekeepers' (c. 1826), 'Bad laws said he are lawless food / To feed a tyrants appetite / I will but reverence the good / & break thro wrong to get at right'.[30]

Clare wasn't the only *London Magazine* writer drawn to the Robin Hood stories. Two years before Clare's first visit to the metropolis, a trip that involved seeing the outlaw on stage in a hastily concocted version of Walter Scott's *Ivanhoe* (1819), J. H. Reynolds began a greenwood-focused exchange with his fellow Cockney poet, John Keats, an exercise in literary sociability that produced a quartet of poems all of which were subsequently known to Clare.[31] Launching what has been called the 'annus mirabilis of Robin Hood literature', Reynolds's opening pair of sonnets 'To a Friend' (February 1818), and Keats's response, delivered both whimsical arcadian fantasy and pithy comment on present social ills.[32] For while Reynolds was happy to imagine a 'merry' forest meeting with 'archer-men in green' and 'Robin at their head, and Marian', Keats's offering was altogether more critical.[33] In his instant reply to Reynolds, the radically dissenting poet found an age when 'men knew nor rent nor leases' reduced to one of 'hard money'. With his sheltering trees felled to build ships 'now rotted on the briny seas', and the honey of wild bees commodified, should an unfortunate Robin (and again Marian) return from the grave 'She would weep, and he would craze'.[34]

Challenged by his friend's deeper engagement with the subject, and with the government's approach to civil liberties then a cause for liberal concern, Reynolds's third, and final, sonnet made explicit the Ritsonite connection between 'Robin, the outlaw' and the 'mass of freedom' still carried by his name.[35] In the shadow of William Hone's recent trial for blasphemous libel, an event which saw Clare's future associate defend himself on the idea of the free-born Englishman, it was important for the legally trained Reynolds – and in Clare's eyes 'one of the best fellows living' – to make clear the Cockney commitment to undying liberty.[36] Published at the end of February in John Hunt's weekly journal *Yellow Dwarf*, and read from by Hazlitt during a lecture at the Surrey Institution, Reynolds's sonnets later appeared in *The Garden of Florence and Other Poems* (1821), a copy of which the author gifted to Clare in the autumn of 1824. Meanwhile, Keats had judged his own Robin Hood strong enough for inclusion in what proved his final collection of poems. Published by Taylor and Hessey in 1820,

Lamia, Isabella, The Eve of St. Agnes and Other Poems was a volume which Clare read closely.

Following the path of his Cockney protégés, John Hunt's better-known brother, Leigh Hunt, likewise found his way to the 'outlaw bold' in his four 'Songs of Robin Hood' (1820). While Leigh Hunt's greenwood sociability suggests the influence of Reynolds, by working through the garland themes of broken forest laws and reprisals against the 'haughty rich', the leader of the Regency equivalent of the literary left made his own contribution to these urban Robin Hoods.[37] Thus, if the *Reliques* licensed Clare to employ the tales of his youth in developing his art, a combination of Reynolds, Keats and Hunt opened the way for Taylor's later suggestion of an 'improved Robin Hood'. Part of this project, at least as Clare saw it, was to make the hero of old speak more directly to the present. One way to do this was to have Robin and his band fight with gamekeepers not foresters and cut out the Marianizing – though Keats, as we have seen, had used the feminine presence to good modernizing effect. In a way that Clare doubtless intended, lines such as 'The game they are a lawless breed / That keep no bounds to feed upon / They trespass upon all to feed / & are for all as well as one' have more of the nineteenth century about them than the twelfth or thirteenth. The point is further emphasized by the presence of 'majistrate laws' and the staging, albeit with bows and arrows, of a full-bloodied poaching affray.[38] And as with the poachers of his own day – of whom some even took the outlaw's name – Clare's men of Sherwood were as determined to have pheasants and hares as a 'good fat buck or doe'.[39]

'They make a prison of the forrest': Protest and Performance

Riding through Surrey in the autumn of 1825 William Cobbett recorded how 'the great business of life in the country, appertains, in some way or other, to the game'.[40] Much given to eye-catching hyperbole, on this occasion the great chronicler of rural life in the troubled decade before Captain Swing was not exaggerating. Though Clare's opinion of Cobbett moved between respect for his 'powerful prose' to general distrust of its purpose, he would certainly have shared this view.[41] For while Clare, like Cobbett, found some virtue in the colourful display of fox-hunting, there was nothing good to be said for the shooting of game. To be sure, the hunt might attract such undesirable parish types as Farmer Cheetum or the whoring young squire Headlong Racket, but it

One of a series of eight prints entitled *The Poacher's Progress*. No. 4,
'Snaring Pheasants'. Charles Turner (1825-6).

did not entail the physical and legal enclosure of land and selected
wild animals into socially exclusive preserves.[42] Along with any
political objection Clare might hold against this increasingly
fashionable pursuit, equally important were the impacts on his
everyday life-space. In other words, if the shooting of game and
the laws underpinning it created numerous social flashpoints at an
already difficult time, for outward-looking countrymen like Clare
they intersected both local and national concerns. In the same year
that Cobbett made the observation noted above, Clare made the
following entry in his journal:

> Took a walk in the fields a birds nesting and botanizing and had like
> to be taken up as a poacher in Hillywood by a meddlesome conseited
> keeper belonging to Sir John Trollop he swore that he had seen me in
> the act more than once of shooting game [...] what terryfying rascals
> these wood keepers and gamekeepers are they make a prison of the
> forrests and are its joalers.[43]

And for 9 September 1824:

> Took a pleasant walk today in the fields but felt too weak to keep out
> long tis the first day of shooting with the sportsmen and the poor
> hares partridges and pheasants were flying in all directions panic
> struck they put me in mind of the inhabitants of a Village flying
> before an invading enemy[44]

In addition to restricting Clare's precious access to the natural
world the preservation of game was instrumental in its organized
destruction. From the early lines 'crowing pheasant in the brakes
[who] Betrays his lair wi awkward squawls / A certain aim the
gunner takes / He clumbsy fluskers up and falls', to the later lines
'The coveys rise – the sportsman joys / & in the stubbles bleeding
fall', the cruelty described varied little.[45] But if the 'brazen murders'
committed by Headlong Racket and his kind were not bad enough,
further adding to Clare's antipathy was the human cost – a cost as
he viewed it paid largely by men of his own class who 'honest of
all other matters' were proscribed in law as poachers and treated as
if 'they had stolen the crown of England'.[46] Given such views, and
his stated dislike of gamekeepers, it's easy to understand another
ballad tradition that Clare embraced – and which later song-
collectors placed firmly in the context of lost common rights – that
of the bold or gallant poacher.[47]

As Clare's recourse to both suggests, from Robin Hood in
his Lincoln Green to the moonlit delights of 'The Lincolnshire
Poacher' was a relatively short step. Recorded in William Chappell's
1840 collection of *National English Airs* as 'well known amongst
the peasantry' (it was also well known on the London stage), it
celebrates the companionable pleasures of illicit hunting 'in the
season of the year'.[48] The Lincolnshire poacher, or whatever his
county variant, never went out alone and he never got caught.
Fond of lively evenings of drinking and song at the dilapidated
cottage known as Bachelors' Hall, its likely appeal for Clare and his
convivial hosts John and James Billings is clear. Game is snared,
keepers are bested, money is made and loyalties are forged: 'We sold
him for a crown, me boys, but I did not tell you where'.[49]

According to Frederick Martin's account, these laddish nights
at the Hall were partly funded by cash made from poaching, an
idea refuted by Clare in a promotional sketch of his life written for
Taylor in 1821. Taking issue with the 'snarling mischief-makers
who would feignly belye me' [...] as stealing Game etc', his non-

The Poacher's Progress. No. 6,
'Scuffling with the Constables in the Skittle Grounds'.

involvement in such 'depredations' was indignantly insisted upon.[50] Later, however, Clare did recall a poaching expedition undertaken one Sunday with the Billings brothers in around 1814-15. On this somewhat farcical occasion the hapless trio's gun 'bursted' before they could bag any game, and in a moment that might have come from one of the period's numerous cautionary tales against poaching a shaken Clare vowed never again to attempt such a mission.[51]

In a manner established by the Tibbles, it is customary for Clare's biographers to note the wisdom of this decision as under 'laws of such severity' a convicted poacher might face 'imprisonment, public whipping, hard labour and even transportation'.[52] Although prior to their reform in 1831 the game laws came with a fearsome-looking assemblage of keepers, spring-guns, mantraps and various types of incarceration, all backed by a 'Holy Alliance' of implacable magistrates and squires, their operational severity should not be pushed too far.[53] For instance, such was the disquiet at the Night Poaching Act of 1816 with its mandatory punishment of seven years' transportation that it had to be modified within a year and was further amended in 1828. In the previous year spring-guns and mantraps had been banned and the poaching-related clauses of the Black Act repealed. By this point public whipping, which only ever applied to night poachers on a second offence, had not been used for over a decade, and of the 1700 men liable for transportation between 1817 and 1828 less than 10% actually suffered this fate. Ballads like 'Van Diemen's Land' told a truth, but not the whole story.[54]

To put it another way, if Clare had been caught poaching on the occasion described in his unfinished autobiography the most likely outcome would have been a £5 fine or three months' jail in lieu of payment. Should he have been 'taken up as a poacher' when innocently botanizing in 1825, a £5 fine would again have been the typical outcome. Like many in his position Clare understandably resented the attentions of keepers, and disliked what they represented, but if he ever went 'in terror' of them it was as much his own imagining as daily fact of life.[55] To meet the demand for more game the number of keepers was steadily growing, but compared to the 17,000 plus recorded on the eve of WWI, when the largest bags were counted in the thousands rather than at most a few hundred, the *c.* 3,000 registered in the 1820s meant that countrywide 'at least half the fields and woods never knew the attentions of gamekeepers'.[56] This was more so the case in counties like Northamptonshire where hunting was generally favoured over shooting.

Whatever the situation on the ground, one way for Clare not to be scared of the keeper, and to safely protest at 'tyrant knaves that made the laws / To keep the cowards slaves', was to write himself into Robin Hood's band of outlaws or otherwise become the member of a close-knit gang of poachers.[57] To write poems like 'Robin & the Gamekeepers' and 'The Poachers' was both to try and 'improve' upon traditions he greatly admired and to engage with subjects of obvious contemporary interest. Around the same time, other labouring-class poets such as John Nicholson of Airedale, and the Nottinghamshire stocking-weaver Robert Millhouse, were writing of poachers and Robin Hood, whilst in 1829 the Corn Law Rhymer, Ebenezer Elliot, was noting how the fiercely independent Jem the Poacher 'begs not [but] feeds on partridge, because bread is dear'.[58] But for Clare to write on these subjects was not just to be relevant, it was to perform and exhibit resistance through the best means available to him. In becoming the 'hero of his own chapbook'

Clare could not only work through his fears and resentments but could also put himself and his imaginary comrades firmly on the side of freedom.[59]

By having the first word of 'The Poachers' as 'Come', Clare draws us immediately into the world of his subject and a whole tradition of broadside balladry. From 'The Saucy Sailor Boy' to 'The Gallant Poachers' (c. 1820), this invitingly instructional verb provided a classic opening to the form.[60] In this case Clare makes it the opening to a song with which the 'chief of the poacher band' regales (and instructs) his men, an echo perhaps of Clare's time in the militia: 'Come prime your guns your belts throw on'.[61] Staying in genre mode we are then given the best-known lines from 'The Lincolnshire Poacher': '& a shining night is our delight / At the season of the year'.[62] From the sensual pleasures of poaching we move through the moral justification of 'freedom in our cause' and back to the practicalities of being properly armed: 'For the sound of the Gun as sure as fate / Is the death knell of the game'.[63] With the poacher-chief's song thus concluded we know we are in serious territory, a long way from sentimental accounts of the village

The Poacher's Progress. No. 7, 'Before the Magistrate'.

poacher found in Mary Russell Mitford's then popular sketches of country life.[64] As Clare presents it, this is just the kind of poaching – armed, in a gang, and at night – that brought the full weight of the game laws to bear, and which in 1827 led to a fatal affray in Rockingham Forest when a man from Corby was speared in the stomach by one of the Earl of Winchelsea's keepers.[65]

Beyond what he heard or read about, this was also the kind of poaching about which Clare, and most other rural inhabitants, knew little. Yet as with his accounts of gypsies where there is necessarily both distance and closeness, the literary sustaining the experiential, the atmosphere of the piece – its implied tenseness amid the 'Carousing' in the Robin-Hood style forest cave – carries its own kind of authenticity.[66] Partly this is a world that the physically unimpressive and night-fearing Clare is fantasizing over (a kind of Bachelors' Hall with serious criminal intent), but it is also one he is detailing with some accuracy. The connection between male drinking culture and poaching, also evident in 'The Gallant Poachers', has since been made by historians, while the repeated reference to guns is a sharp reminder of how limited their control then was. This in turn relates to a lively ongoing debate over the right to bear arms as a means of self-defence and as a crucial guard against state-imposed tyranny. Soon to be taken up by Chartists in articles such as 'The Game Laws, A Nefarious Measure for Keeping the People in Subjection', this debate is clearly being voiced in 'The Poachers'.[67]

In the poem's final verse the poachers set off on their night's work. In contrast to his tale of Robin Hood, in which the outlaws easily get the better of the 'lusty keepers', the outcome here feels less assured.[68] Similar to 'The Gallant Poachers', and indeed to Crabbe's ultimately tragic 'Smugglers and Poachers', not all of the men will make it back. Mirroring the fate of the game to be hunted: 'The storm approached the winds did blow / Some comrades funeral knell / But no one paused or cared to know / What day would have to tell'.[69] Here the narrative ends, but for closure we can look to 'Robin Hood & the Gamekeepers' and the 'wailing mothers' left to mourn those lost in 'the fray'.[70] Whether it be keepers grieved over or poachers, at the height of the game-law conflict the casualties mounted on both sides. Whatever the politics of those who legislated, bad laws – as Clare saw it – would always produce grievous outcomes.

At the end of 1826 Clare's growing family enjoyed a festive dinner of pheasant. Courtesy of the Exeters it had come from an estate on which Clare had formerly gone in fear of the keepers. He had trespassed there because as a young labourer living in cramped surroundings it was a quiet and secluded place for him to develop his craft.[71] Steeped in the garland tales of Robin Hood, and later familiar with a new generation of sociably-produced outlaw poems, as a published writer who now went to Burghley by invite, Clare was ready to take up the challenge issued by Taylor. At the same time his growing interest in song and ballad collection, long-standing dislike of the game laws, and need of manly fellowship, directed him towards the complementary subject of poaching. To be on the side of the poacher was to defy the noticeboard fixing tyrants of enclosure, to assert some independence from patrons, and to call up the spirit of old Robin Hood. Or as his loyal friend and supporter Eliza Emmerson punningly put it, in this he could be more than 'Little John'.[72]

NOTES

1   Christopher Hill, *Liberty Against the Law: Some Seventeenth-Century Controversies* (London: Penguin, 1997), p. 98; Taylor to Clare, quoted in Mina Gorji, 'Clare's "Merry England"', *JCSJ*, 24 (2005), 12.
2   Margaret Grainger, *John Clare: Collector of Ballads* (Peterborough Museum Society, 1964), pp. 12-14; George Deacon, *John Clare and the Folk Tradition* (London: Sinclair Browne, 1983), pp. 132-4, 138-40, 164-9; Gorji, 11-15.
3   I understand this poem as dating from around the same time as 'The Gipseys Song' and 'Robin Hood and the Gamekeepers'.
4   John Clare, *A Champion of the Poor: Political Verse and Prose*, ed. by P.M.S. Dawson, Eric Robinson and David Powell (Ashington: Carcanet Press, 2000), pp. 122-9 and 120-1. This collection has 'the priest of Lorn' as 'Boys bring booty from the cave'. *Middle Period*, IV, p. 396, l. 25.
5   'The Gipseys Song' appeared in the *European Magazine* in 1825. *Middle Period*, IV, p. 53, l. 15; p. 55, l. 75.
6   'The Village Minstrel', *Early Poems*, II, p. 168, l. 1052.
7   Bate, *Biography*, pp. 218-19; 'The Village Minstrel', *Early Poems*, II, p. 169, ll. 1086-8.
8   'The Milton Hunt', *Early Poems*, II, p. 199, ll. 17 and 24.
9   'The Village Minstrel', *Early Poems*, II, p. 79, l. 156.
10   Before 1831 the basic legal qualification to shoot game was the ownership of land with an annual rental value of £100: 50 times what was required to vote for a county MP.
11   Thomas Bewick, *A Memoir of Thomas Bewick* (Oxford University Press, 1975), p. 170.
12   George Crabbe, 'Smugglers and Poachers', in *Tales of the Hall* (London: John Murray, 1819), p. 306.
13   Ibid., p. 325. In 1822 Clare was presented with a copy of Crabbe's works by Lord Milton. Clare was equally dismissive of the evangelical writings of Hannah More – especially it seems her moralizing fable of the good-for-nothing poacher Black Giles. See Deacon, pp. 33-4.

14 Matthew Cragoe and Briony McDonagh, 'Parliamentary enclosure, vermin and the cultural life of English parishes, 1750-1850', *Continuity and Change*, 28.1 (2013), 37-8.

15 *By Himself*, p. 84; Hill, p. 98.

16 James C. Scott, *Weapons of the Weak: Everyday Forms of Peasant Resistance* (New Haven: Yale University Press, 1985), p. 265. On Michel de Certeau's theory of 'tactics' as they might relate to Clare see Simon Kövesi, *John Clare: Nature, Criticism and History* (London: Palgrave Macmillan, 2017), pp. 18-20.

17 Bridget Keegan, *British Labouring-Class Nature Poetry, 1730-1837* (Basingstoke: Palgrave Macmillan, 2008), p. 179.

18 'The Shepherd's Calendar' (November), *Middle Period*, I, p. 150, l. 117. According to village lore a bow found at nearby Woodcroft Castle had once belonged to Robin Hood.

19 John Goodridge and Kelsey Thornton, *John Clare The Trespasser* (Nottingham: Five Leaves Publications, 2016); John Lucas, *England and Englishness: Ideas of Nationhood in English Poetry, 1688-1900* (London: Hogarth Press, 1990), chp. 7; Roger Sales, *John Clare: A Literary Life* (Basingstoke: Palgrave, 2002), p. 28.

20 Quoted in Leslie Shepard, *The History of Street Literature* (Newton Abbot: David & Charles, 1973), p. 114.

21 *By Himself*, p. 57.

22 On the development of the Robin Hood stories see R.B. Dobson and John Taylor, *Rymes of Robin Hood: An Introduction to the English Outlaw* (Stroud: Sutton Publishing, 1989). 'The Woodman', *Early Poems*, II, pp. 294-5, ll. 184-7.

23 *Early Poems*, II, p. 162, ll. 934-5.

24 Bate, *Biography*, p. 57. The aristocratic outlaw, usually the dispossessed Earl of Huntingdon, was not part of the garland tradition but largely the invention of the Elizabethan playwright Anthony Munday. Munday also helped introduce the character of Maid Marian.

25 Quoted in Sales, p. 39.

26 Ibid. In a failed attempt to deter commercial poaching the purchase of game was made illegal in 1818. Jack i' the Green was the nickname given to Clare by Thomas Hood.

27 Quoted in Shepard, p.114.

28 *Letters*, p. 82.

29 Joseph Ritson, *Robin Hood: A Collection of All the Ancient Poems, Songs and Ballads* (Wakefield: EP Publishing, 1972), pp. vi, xii-xiii. This is a reprint of the 1823 edition, the same edition Clare acquired the following year.

30 *Middle Period*, IV, p. 426, ll. 69-72.

31 J.W. and Anne Tibble, *John Clare: A Life* (London: Michael Joseph, 1972), p. 119. In *Ivanhoe* Robin Hood appears as the Saxon freedom-fighter Locksley.

32 Dobson and Taylor, p. 199. 1818 saw Scott begin *Ivanhoe* and Thomas Love Peacock complete most of his satirical novella, *Maid Marian*.

33 Quoted in John Barnard, 'Keats's "Robin Hood", John Hamilton Reynolds, and the Old Poets', *Proceedings of the British Academy*, LXXV (1989), 183-4.

34 Quoted in Nicholas Roe, *John Keats and the Culture of Dissent* (Oxford: Clarendon Press, 1997), pp. 149-50.

35 Quoted in Barnard, 193.

36 *By Himself*, p. 141.

37   Leigh Hunt, 'How Robin and his Outlaws lived in the Woods', in *The Selected Writings of Leigh Hunt: Poetical Works, 1801-21*, ed. by John Strachan (London: Pickering and Chatto, 2003), p. 197, l. 53; Jeffrey N. Cox, *Poetry and Politics in the Cockney School: Keats, Shelley, Hunt and their Circle* (Cambridge University Press, 2004), p. 39.

38   'Robin Hood & the Gamekeepers', *Middle Period*, IV, p. 426, ll. 73-6; p. 424, l. 33.

39   *Middle Period*, IV, p. 426, l. 85. For example, Love Peacock's *Maid Marian* was partly inspired by the anti-enclosure poachers of Windsor Forest who in 1813 adopted the names of Robin Hood and his men.

40   William Cobbett, *Rural Rides* (Harmondsworth: Penguin, 1979), pp. 242-3.

41   Bate, *Biography*, p. 358.

42   John Clare, *The Parish: A Satire*, ed. by Eric Robinson (London: Penguin Classics, 1986), pp. 40-1, ll. 381-409; p. 38, ll. 281-306. Clare's feelings towards fox-hunting were not entirely unmixed, see Anne Barton, 'Clare's Animals: The Wild and the Tame', *JCSJ*, 18 (1999), 5-21.

43   *By Himself*, p. 222.

44   Ibid., p. 172.

45   'Autumn', *Early Poems*, II, p. 79, ll. 149-52; quoted in Barton, 12. In early correspondence Clare sometimes referred to himself as the 'pheasant poet'.

46   *The Parish*, p. 38, l. 302; see *Champion for the Poor*, p. xxiii.

47   A. L. Lloyd, *The Singing Englishman: An Introduction to Folksong* (London: Workers' Music Association, 1944), pp. 48-9.

48   William Chappell, *A Collection of English Airs: Consisting of Ancient Song, Ballad and Dance Tunes* (London: Chappell, 1840), p. 62.

49   *Folksongs of Britain and Ireland*, ed. by Peter Kennedy (London: Cassell, 1975), pp. 568-9. Kennedy gives the Northamptonshire variant.

50   Frederick Martin, *The Life of John Clare* (London: Frank Cass, 1964), p. 43; *By Himself*, p. 25.

51   *By Himself*, p. 52.

52   Tibbles, p. 68; Bate, *Biography*, p. 99.

53   J. L. and Barbara Hammond, *The Village Labourer* (Longmans: London, 1913), p. 188. The reforms of 1831, which on paper at least made shooting a less socially restricted pastime, owed much to one of Clare's principal patrons Lord Althorp.

54   See Peter Munsche, *Gentleman and Poachers: The English Game Laws, 1671-1831* (Cambridge University Press, 1981).

55   Goodridge and Thornton, p. 27.

56   F. M. L. Thompson, 'Landowners and the rural community', in *The Unquiet Countryside*, ed. by G. E. Mingay (London: Routledge, 1989), pp. 84-5.

57   'The Poachers', *Middle Period*, IV, p. 378, ll. 15-16.

58   John Nicholson, 'The Poacher', in *Airedale in Ancient Times* (London: Seeley and Son, 1825); Robert Millhouse, *Sherwood Forest and Other Poems* (London, 1827); Ebenezer Elliot, 'The Village Patriarch', in *Selected Poetry of Ebenezer Elliot*, ed. by Mark Storey (Madison: Fairleigh Dickinson University Press, 2008), p. 57. In 1838 Clare's friend, Allan Cunningham, wrote a series of articles on Robin Hood for Charles Knight's *Penny Magazine*.

59   *By Himself*, p. x.

60   *The New Penguin Book of English Folk Songs*, ed. by Steve Roud and Julia Bishop (London: Penguin, 2012), pp. 40-41, 334-6.

61 *Middle Period*, IV, p. 378, l. 1; p. 379, l. 25.

62 *Middle Period*, IV, p. 378, ll. 11-12.

63 *Middle Period*, IV, p. 378, l. 13; p. 379, ll. 23-4.

64 Mary Russell Mitford, *Our Village: Sketches of Rural Character and Scenery* (London: Geo. B. Whittaker, 1826).

65 *News From the English Countryside, 1750-1850*, ed. by Clifford Morsley (London: Harrap, 1979), p. 232.

66 *Middle Period*, IV, p. 379, l. 26; Sarah Houghton-Walker, 'Clare's Gypsies and Literary Influence', *JCSJ*, 28 (2009), 71-93.

67 *Chartist Circular*, 18 January 1840, p. 1. In theory the game laws made the possession of firearms by those not qualified to shoot unlawful, but this made little difference to actual possession which itself was enabled under the 1689 Bill of Rights

68 *Middle Period*, IV, p. 426, l. 91.

69 *Middle Period*, IV, p. 379, ll. 37-40.

70 *Middle Period*, IV, p. 430, l. 163; p. 428, l. 122.

71 *By Himself*, p. 100.

72 Quoted in Bate, *Biography*, p. 306.

Study for 'The Ferry', Peter De Wint (1784–1849), after 1829, watercolour and graphite. The Metropolitan Museum of Art, New York.

A Length of Road:
Interview with Robert Hamberger

Simon Kövesi

Robert Hamberger has published four poetry collections. His latest, 'Blue Wallpaper', was shortlisted for the 2020 Polari Prize. In 1995 Robert retraced John Clare's 1841 walk of eighty-five miles from High Beach asylum to his home in Northborough. His first non-fiction book *A Length of Road: Finding myself in the footsteps of John Clare*, and the occasion for this interview, describes the experience of this walk at a time of personal crisis, reflecting on, and contrasting with, Clare's journey. It was published by John Murray in June 2021. The book is genre-fluid: part memoir, part nature writing, part literary criticism, with twenty-eight poems in Clare's voice and the voices of those he met on his walk. It is an exploration of class, gender, family, friendship, grief and sexuality through the author's own experiences and the autobiographical writing of John Clare. This interview was conducted by correspondence between Robert Hamberger and Simon Kövesi across April and May 2021. The interview is followed by a few sample poems from *A Length of Road*.

Simon Kövesi: What drew you to John Clare for this project?

Robert Hamberger: John Clare is one of a few writers who seems to have followed me through various parts of my life. In *A Length of Road* I write about how I was first introduced to him at the age of fifteen, when my Art teacher in our Bethnal Green grammar school lent me a book of his poems. I hadn't heard of him before then. I loved his poems, their direct beauty had a real impact on me. I called them 'true poetry' in my teenage journal at the time. I think maybe if you're introduced to a great writer at a susceptible age they stay with you, almost become a talisman. I remember seeing Hilton's portrait of him at The National Portrait Gallery sometime shortly after that, and it's such a starry image of a poet, staring ahead as if he's inspired. For an arty teenager with ambitions to write such images stay with you. I moved from London to Northamptonshire when I married in the late seventies, as my wife came from Northamptonshire. Clare was then (and probably still is) very much seen as Northamptonshire's poet, so I visited his birthplace (years before it was a museum) and I want to say how much his biography gets mixed up with his poetry: this peasant poet who became an overnight success, took trips to London, stayed besotted with his first love Mary and ended up in Northampton Asylum. For a working-class writer like myself I think there's something almost like an intriguing warning in Clare's story: the dangers of 'literature' for working-class writers. I don't think that's logical or thought out, but I'd suggest there's something mythical and emblematic in Clare for working-class writers. I only found out about his walk from the asylum in Epping Forest towards his home a year or so before I retraced it in 1995. When I read his marvellous journal of the walk I was bowled over, and knew instinctively I wanted to retrace it. That certainly wasn't thought out either, as regards the practical obstacles of eighty-five miles in four days; trying to keep as much as possible to his route along the Great North Road, as far as I understood it then. But I knew I wanted to retrace it, and sleep rough as he did, and try to write about the experience, as a tribute to him, to put myself in his shoes, if that might at all be possible.

SK: What do you think happens to Clare's poetry and prose, and to you as a reader, once you have 'experienced' its places first-hand, as it were? And how did these places impact you as a writer?

RH: One of Clare's beauties is that he is a tremendously immediate writer. We're beside him, for example, in his brilliant Northborough sonnets. We hush when he tells us, and 'part aside / These hazel branches' with him as we approach 'The Nightingale's Nest'. Of course I now read the journal of his walk differently since I experienced those eighty-five miles in my pores and the soles of my feet. I agree with Iain Sinclair that Clare's 'Journey out of Essex' is 'one of the wonders of English prose.' He writes in such a visceral way about the exhaustion and disorientation of long distance walking, and I tried to capture some of that in writing about my walk, tried to make the reader feel the blisters, so to speak. It's one reason I kept the walk in the present tense: not only because I was speaking into a dictaphone as I walked, but because Clare somehow shows us how the act of walking can feel eternally present in a walking body. Clare's account reminds me of Werner Herzog's book 'Of Walking in Ice' about his 1974 walk from Munich to Paris, a book that was helpful to me when I was drafting *A Length of Road*. On my retracing I think I may have found the milestone Clare refers to at Jack's Hill ('the last Mile stone 35 Miles from London') and even if I'm wrong, it was magical to feel the whiff of his presence, or kid myself I could. There's a similar sense of him permeating Helpston, Glinton and Northborough I think, and his writing helps me reconsider that landscape, which is unfamiliar to me. It's not that Clare made his mark in those villages and fields. Somehow he's too secretive a writer for that – or he refuses to place himself above or beyond the landscape. Maybe we still sense his attentiveness and commemoration of those places through his poems. One of the things Clare teaches us is that sights that could be dismissed as mundane or run-of-the-mill have significance if we pay attention, and that's always useful for a writer to remember: simply observe.

SK: In this book, you document how you have followed Clare's tracks in geographical – even biographical – ways. I wonder how or whether you see yourself as an heir to Clare, in stylistic, technical or linguistic terms? Do you think his art has informed your own? And are there other writers who have had similar impacts on your own art?

RH: I'd like to suggest that any contemporary working-class writer might be seen as an heir to Clare, because his example of perseverance, staying true to his vision and language despite financial and artistic pressures, is so important. On the other hand, it may feel a little presumptuous of me to claim myself as one of his heirs. Our subject matter is totally different, as I don't usually focus that closely on nature in most of my poetry, though Clare's example helped me to focus on the nature and wildlife I encountered during my walk, and I tried to develop that in my poems in *A Length of Road*. I think Clare has taught me in two fundamental ways. The first is that we share a love of sonnets. I'm not half as inventive in sonnet forms as Clare. My rhyme-schemes stick pretty rigidly to Shakespearean and Petrarchan forms, and I experiment with unrhymed sonnets, whereas his playfulness with original sonnet rhyme-schemes is daring and impressive. But that immediacy I mentioned earlier in his writing is in full display in his sonnets. Any sonneteer can learn a great deal from him. The second lesson I learned from Clare I'm still learning, and that's through what I might term his honest use of language. Unlike Clare, I don't use dialect in my poems, but I have what I'd call a political belief in trying to write as directly, as simply, as possible in my poems, so that my poems could be accepted – and (hopefully) responded to – by people who may not usually be experts in contemporary poetry, or may be put off by linguistic gymnastics or ironic distance or complex references. Trying to write as simply as I can feels like an aesthetic choice based on my working-class origins, so I would say that Clare has influenced me – and continues to influence me – in those terms. Other writers who have had complementary influences on my art are queer American writers like Adrienne Rich and Mark Doty. I love Rich's fierce political engagement and Doty's lyricism and unashamed focus on the self. I've learned from them both about using the scrutiny of an autobiographical lens as frankly as possible in my poetry and my memoir.

SK: You are open and very detailed about your personal relationships in this book. What do you think are the risks and the benefits – to you both as a private person and also as a public artist, and to us as readers – of such closely confessional literature?

RH: The drafting of my memoir took place – on and off – over twenty-five years, since my retracing of Clare's walk happened in 1995. There was a great deal of hesitation, self-doubt and self-sabotage during its various drafts, as well as feeling that no-one may be interested in my story, that it was potentially arrogant of an unknown working-class poet both to write about Clare and to place my life centre-stage. So for those years of drafting part of me was convinced that the book wouldn't be published anyway. This meant I had to write it primarily for myself, to use the memoir as an attempt to make sense of my experience, whatever had happened in my life to lead me to the point of my four-day walk. It meant confronting the artistic risks of honesty (as much as possible) and self-examination, self-judgement. Of course part of me kept half an eye on the possibility of future publication, so although many of the details might feel to a reader like radical self-exposure there were some aspects of my life I've chosen not to share in the book. Memoir is a paradox, in that it's an apparently private form in a public forum. Yet reading is essentially a private act: just the author and the reader. So I need to speak intimately to the reader for the memoir to feel valid. I need to confess my vulnerabilities and my sins, and hope that by doing so an act of empathy might happen. The reader might feel 'I have felt that, or something similar. I've made similar mistakes and errors, been similarly confused or depressed.' I'm a pro-feminist writer, so I believe the personal is political. Although you could argue that men have told their stories *ad nauseam*, I wanted to unpeel the public mask of masculinity. I felt it was important to try and admit vulnerability, fallibility. For example, the end of a marriage is unfortunately all too common, but I think it might help others in similar crises to hear a man speak honestly about his mess of feelings when a long love ends. As we know with the high rate of male suicides, men still have damaging difficulties in admitting vulnerability, talking about their mental health, even trying to voice their confusions and fears, because it's still seen as a sign of

Robert Hamberger, 2021

weakness within both patriarchy and capitalism. As men, I think we have to counter that self-destructive message by speaking as honestly as possible about our fears and so-called weakness, about how important love and friendships are to us, how we need to understand our sexuality and any misogyny in ourselves, how we want to retain close relationships with our children. Before publication my family read the manuscript and I would never have included anything in the book that they were unhappy about. I made that clear to them when the book was accepted for publication. I think that respect for the people depicted in the book is crucial, and for those people in the book who have since died, I felt all I could do was honour their memory and complexity as best I could. I only have the right to tell my own story, not theirs, and to assume nothing about their motives or feelings or actions. To me memoirs are essentially about empathy, so it's worth taking personal and artistic risks to achieve the possibility of connection, to make it real.

SK: Towards the end of *A Length of Road*, you ask 'What can I trust in this new loneliness?' In the end, is the act of reaching out and tracking Clare in such intimate and self-revelatory detail working to form an act of poetic community, or does it rather serve to reinscribe the complete loneliness and isolation of both Clare and you, as a contemporary pilgrim poet? Does reading Clare make us more lonely?

RH: What an intriguing question! I say early on in *A Length of Road* that my retracing of Clare's walk is a clumsy attempt to 'claim kinship' with Clare, while admitting I have no right to do so. I think working-class and other marginalised writers – who don't necessarily see their lives reflected or represented in books – may have an instinctive need to hunt for models, for those who've blazed a trail before us from similar circumstances, no matter how full of confusion, error and difference those earlier examples may be. We can learn from them – we probably need to – about their strategies for perseverance, how they kept writing. I believe that Clare blazed a trail for all writers who are working-class or from rural communities or who may have experienced mental illness or who are acutely aware of the risks to, and beauties of, nature. That's a wide remit – and a pretty cumbersome burden for him – but his writing covered all those fields, along with loads of others. I think we're only just starting to properly celebrate Clare for the wide-ranging writer he was. Shifting him closer towards the traditional canon of English poetry feels like a way for the literary establishment to begin to acknowledge how narrow it has been historically, as regards which writers and perspectives are allowed into that canon. I feel on the margins of contemporary English poetry for a range of reasons, including my class origins, my sexuality and the unfashionable approach I take to poetry. But I feel that writing this book was an attempt to create a poetic community, not only with Clare, but with under-represented writers who may have similar origins, face similar dilemmas. To push beyond the working-class pressure to self-censor. We see Clare attempted that breaking of boundaries in sometimes alarming ways, in facing his own misogyny in *Don Juan*, for instance. I acknowledge that the need to create a writing community often comes from a place of isolation or loneliness, but I think the attempt to do so is admirable – it's worth making. In my poem 'Unpacking the Books' I call writers our 'paper companions' and I believe writers can help to reduce our isolation. An example from Clare is probably his most famous line 'I am – yet what I am, none cares or knows'. Its fame shows that it resonates down the generations. Why? Because he found precise words for an isolation (or even desolation) that many of us might have caught a whisker of in our own experiences. So, for me, reading Clare can help us feel less lonely, more connected, both to nature and to aspects of experience – including love of course. It might be helpful to end with Clare's amazing statement in Northampton Asylum that I quote and explore on the night of returning to my rented room after my walk: 'sometimes they called me Shakespeare and sometimes Byron and sometimes Clare'. I sense that might have been Clare's attempt to express how poetry moves even across individual identities. So if we start from isolation or loneliness we could move towards the possibility of dissolving our distinctions, of creating the potential for communities and communication between writers, even across time. I agree with Clare about the honourable nature of making such an attempt.

Three Poems from *A Length of Road*

MOVEMENT

July 20 Reconnitred the route the Gipsey pointed out & found it a
legible one to make a movement & having only honest courage &
myself in my army I led the way & my troops soon followed

I'm squint-eye flap-arm Nelson
puffing up sails as the wind blows,
squashing frogs like scummy jailers
quacks and whores and poxy printers.
If my head's whacked off by a cannonball
I can glue it back again.

Slow down lad. You're Random Jack,
simply aiming home. I've fallen on that word
and live to breathe under clouds I still remember,
to lift my children's waists between my hands –
raise them over my crown and carry them down again,
resting their butterfly's eyelash at the side of my smile.

Her arms will end my wilderness,
hedge me inside to graze her grass.
She'll turn when I knock the kissing-gate.
I'm barred from bee-tickled blades,
until a tongue slipped through her parted teeth
wets mine.

A TALL GYPSY

*I saw a tall Gipsey come out of the Lodge gate & make down the road
…I got up and went on to the next town with her – she cautioned
me on the way to put something in my hat to keep the crown up &
said in a lower tone 'You'll be noticed,' but not knowing what she
hinted I took no notice and made no reply.*

She speaks:

> I live this skin, wanting no other:
> not to be some milk-face supping indoors.
> They quake politely when I read their smiles
> as if I'll blab which husband bores, who dies tomorrow.

> We side with each other
> for ten furlongs into town,
> talk of heading north and why swifts won't land
> before I warn his gawky look.

> Ape them or you'll be noticed.
> Straighten your hat. Stiffen its crown
> and you can skip their questions.
> Take a short cut. Drop the road you're on.

NOTHING

July 24 1841. Returned home out of Essex & found no Mary her &
her family are nothing to me now - though she herself was once the
dearest of all – and how can I forget

Cut my brain in half and pluck her out:
this woman where thought should be,
stooping to touch the cowslips.

I carry myself like spilt wine,
my cup cracked
with the memory of whoever I was.

You can live on so little.
Live on this breath leaving my mouth again,
the song of a robin before it flies.

John Clare's Reception in Germany in the Nineteenth Century

Jens Peters

John Clare's reception in the English-speaking world has varied since the publication of his first volume of poems in 1820. Initial success was followed by a steady decline of readership during the poet's lifetime, a first rediscovery in the late Victorian era and a growing popularity during the late twentieth and early twenty-first centuries. However, it is largely unknown if and how his poetry was received in other countries, especially non-English-speaking ones. This essay is going to take a first step in elucidating this question by looking at Clare's reception in Germany. At first glance, Clare seems to be more or less unknown here, especially in comparison to contemporaries like Byron, whose impact on German literature and society, particularly in the nineteenth century, was immense. The predominance of Byron in the German reception of British Romantic literature can be seen in the fact that it became common usage to refer to this literary period as the 'Age of Byron'.[1] Yet a closer look reveals that, astonishingly, there has indeed been such a thing as a reception of Clare's writings in Germany. This essay focuses on the reception of the poet in Germany during Clare's lifetime.

In the nineteenth century, English had come to rival French as the main foreign language and cultural influence in Germany due to the growing importance of Great Britain in global trade and politics. The growth of interest in English literature can be measured by the university lectures dedicated to this topic. In all the time before 1800, there had only been 124 lectures. In the comparatively short period between 1800 and 1825, this rose to 161 and between 1825 and 1850 the staggering number of 629 lectures in English literature had been reached.[2] But did this growing interest extend to John Clare's poetry? In order to answer this question, I will draw on material found in literary magazines, newspaper reviews, encyclopaedia entries and anthologies. The evidence gathered from these sources demonstrates that there was a limited – but within its boundaries

– lively interest in John Clare who in general seems to have shared the fate of Wordsworth, Keats and other writers from that period:

> Es ist eine auffällige Erscheinung, daß Dichter der Vorromantik wie Thomson, Young und Macpherson sofort und nachhaltig auf ihre kontinentalen Zeitgenossen einwirken konnten, während Cowper, Wordsworth, Shelley oder Keats erst wesentlich später und auch dann noch in beschränktem Umfang auf dem Festland zu Ansehen und Geltung kamen, - offenbar erst dann, als man sich eine Art Wertgefühl für den spezifisch englischen Charakter der insularen romantischen Dichtung erworben hatte.

> (It is noticeable that poets from the pre-Romantic era such as Thomson, Young and Macpherson were able to influence their continental contemporaries immediately and lastingly, whereas Cowper, Wordsworth, Shelley or Keats gained recognition and prestige on the mainland only much later and to a much more limited extent – evidently only when people had developed a kind of appreciation for the specifically English character of the insular Romantic poetry.)[3]

I plan to write a second essay that will trace the further development of such an 'appreciation for [...] insular Romantic poetry' into the twentieth and twenty-first centuries, the latter of which in particular is currently experiencing a strong surge of interest in Clare's writings.

An interpretation of the available material elucidates three tendencies that emerge in the nineteenth century and remain remarkably durable in Clare's reception in Germany:

1) There is a consistent *biographical* interest in his life, often to the detriment of a nuanced perception of his actual writings. In this, German reviewers and journalists follow the implications established by John Taylor's marketing of Clare as a 'peasant poet' in England.

2) This biographical interest often has a *moral* dimension. Clare is taken as an example of a certain class and from his behaviour, lessons can be learned. However, the nature of these lessons undergoes a development from the nineteenth to the twenty-first century.

3) There is a focus on Clare as a writer about the *natural* world and a disregard of most of his other social, political or satirical writing. In the nineteenth century, even this interaction with him as a 'nature poet' remains relatively unspecific, stems more from

his personal background than from his actual writing and is mostly couched in the general terms of landscape poetry and emotions.

The following survey of the material available for the nineteenth century will seek to demonstrate the validity of the three main tendencies of reception I have identified.

First reactions to John Clare

It is surprising to find that John Clare's reception in Germany starts from his very first publication, the *Poems Descriptive*. Only nine months after *Poems Descriptive* had appeared in January 1820 in the UK, the German journal *Das Morgenblatt für gebildete Stände* (*Morning Paper for the Educated Classes*[4]) published on 20 October 1820 in the section 'Englischer Literaturbericht für Juni und Juli 1820' ('Account of English Literature for June and July 1820') a brief account of Clare's life and writings. The anonymous author provides a summary of Octavius Gilchrist's article in *The Quarterly Review* of May of the same year,[5] which he characterises as a 'most tender and sentimental essay' ('äußerst zarter und gefühlvoller Aufsatz').[6] He follows Gilchrist in his focus on Clare's humble and uneducated background, though he radically shortens the account of actual details from Clare's youth. Instead, the author of the German article is more interested in Gilchrist's poetic assessment and his comparison of Clare to Burns and Bloomfield. He translates verbatim the central characterisation of Clare's poetry found in the *Quarterly Review* article:

> He looks abroad with the eye of a poet, and with the minuteness of a naturalist, but the intelligence which he gains is always referred to the heart; it is thus that the falling leaves become admonishers and friends, the idlest weed has its resemblance in his own lowly lot, and the opening primrose of spring suggests the promise that his own long winter of neglect and obscurity will yet be succeeded by a summer's sun of happier fortune.[7]

The only noticeable difference in the translation from the original article lies in the first sentence, which reads in German as follows: 'Seine Gedichte atmen das reinste und frommste Gefühl, einen empfänglichen Sinn für die Reize der Natur'.[8] ('His poems breathe the purest and godliest sentiment, a susceptible sense for the charms of nature.') The German author introduces an element of religious feeling absent in the English original and transforms the quality of a quasi-scientific precision into a more general and effusive 'sensibility'. The article in the *Morgenblatt* is one of the earliest – if not the earliest – mentions of Clare's poetry in Germany and fulfils its role as a general introduction adequately – with two exceptions. In contrast to Gilchrist's article, it fails to mention the name of Clare's first publication and only gives its price (therefore assuming easy access to the original article in case of further interest). And – again in contrast to the original – it does not quote examples from Clare's poetry. The interested German reader with an adequate knowledge of English (which was increasingly more common in the middle and upper classes at the beginning of the nineteenth century) hence has no opportunity to gain a taste of the poetry recommended and to form his or her own assessment. This lack of actual quotations – not to speak of translations – is a feature we will encounter in many other articles dealing with Clare. It contributes considerably to the overall emphasis upon the life in German coverage of Clare, rather than the poetry.

In the same year, Friedrich Johann Jacobsen includes Clare in the appendix to his anthology *Briefe an eine deutsche Edelfrau über die neusten englischen Dichter, herausgegeben mit übersetzten Auszügen vorzüglicher Stellen aus ihren Gedichten und mit den Bildnissen der berühmtesten jetzt lebenden Dichter Englands* ('Letters to a German noblewoman about the latest English poets, published with translated excerpts of exquisite passages from their poems and with pictures of England's most famous living poets').[9] Jacobsen calls Clare a 'blutarmen Bauernknecht' ('anemic farm hand') whose poems are 'von den Recensenten edelmüthig empfohlen' ('generously recommended by the reviewers').[10] Jacobsen provides the title of Clare's first volume of poetry and quotes stanzas 37-40 from the poem 'The Fate of Amy'. He then provides an accurate prose translation of this excerpt. By choosing this cautionary tale as an example of Clare's poetry – a choice reinforced by the focus of the excerpt itself and by the German publication's intended female readership – Jacobsen introduces a moral tone in the reception of Clare that is taken on and developed by subsequent German publications. Like Amy, bit by bit, Clare's own life is turned into a cautionary tale.

A later, much shorter summary in the *Beilage zum literarischen Conversations-Blatt, No. 50* (Supplement to the Literary Conversational Paper[11]), 28 February 1821, that refers to the same original article in the *Quarterly Review*, at least gives the title of Clare's first volume and directs the interested reader explicitly towards the quotations in the English version. Similarly to the earlier article in the *Morgenblatt,* interest is shown in the poet's humble upbringing. The descriptive adjectives in particular demonstrate that the German author reads Clare from a sentimental perspective: he emphasises his 'tiefes und zartes Gefühl' ('deep and tender sentiment') and characterises his style as a 'eben so gemüthvolle als lebhafte Darstellung' ('a depiction both sentimental and lively'). Clare is called a 'Natursänger' ('bard of nature'), thereby similarly highlighting both the seemingly untutored nature of verse (which according to this epithet, comes to him as naturally as song) and his focus on topics taken from nature.[12]

The most extensive piece on Clare published in Germany in the nineteenth century appears in the same publication, the *Literarisches Conversations-Blatt, No 54,* on 5 March 1822. It has the title 'Ein Besuch bei John Clare in dem Dorfe Helpstone in Northamptonshire (Aus dem Briefe eines Reisenden)' ('A visit to John Clare in the village of Helpstone in Northamptonshire [From a traveller's letter]').[13] In contrast to the article in the *Morgenblatt,* no source is named – the article creates the impression of being an original contribution to the magazine. Consequently, contemporary readers must have assumed that the anonymous German writer visited Clare him- or herself. In reality however, the piece is a modified, condensed and rearranged translation of John Taylor's anonymously published article in the *London Magazine,* 'A Visit to John Clare. With a notice of his new poems', of November 1821.[14]

By 1822, just after the publication of his second volume *The Village Minstrel and other Poems,* Clare's reputation in Germany had grown, as the German author's comment in the footnote to the headline shows:

> Von diesem berühmten und beliebten englischen Naturdichter ist auch in deutschen Blättern oftmals die Rede gewesen. Seine Biographie wird das Neue Conversations-Lexicon liefern.[15]

> (This famous and popular English nature poet has been talked about a lot even in German newspapers. *The New Encyclopaedia* will supply his biography.)

The announcement of Clare's forthcoming biography in the same publisher's encyclopaedia (the famous *Brockhaus*)[16] is clearly a marketing ploy, which only makes sense if Clare's name bears sufficient weight to serve as an incentive. For his article, the anonymous German author selects the passages from Taylor's piece describing Helpston as well as the encounter with the poet in his own cottage. He excludes the whole introduction where Taylor meets Clare 'about a mile from home' and walks with him to his cottage via Lolham Brigs and Langley Bush – approximately half of the original.[17] From this passage, only two elements are needed to set the scene for the German reader: firstly, an abbreviated description of Helpston's environs which especially emphasises the industry of its inhabitants ('Fleiß überall' ['diligence everywhere']) that is absent from the original. The local antiquities are also mentioned, but only in passing.[18] Secondly, Clare's wife Patty and her sister, who accompanied him when they are met by the author of the piece, but who agree to go to Casterton to their father-in-law (in this altered context, a journey that had not yet been started).

The result of this curtailing is a focus on the circumstances of Clare's life and a disregard for his poetry in the German article. From the fourteen poems partly or completely quoted in the original, twelve are not included here. The only two that make it into the German article correspond to its focus: the lines describing the elm tree next to his cottage (from 'Address to Plenty, in Winter') and the ones describing his feelings towards his father (from 'Effusion'). Both are quoted in English without a translation. Unlike Taylor, the German author refers a second time to the 'Address to Plenty' by giving its title. The German author then goes on to interpret this poem as literary evidence for the poverty actually encountered in Clare's cottage, and recommends how it does so 'mit herzzerreißender Wahrheit' ('with heartbreaking truthfulness').[19] The poetry is thus subsumed into the German author's own moralising agenda. Taylor's detailed discussion of Clare's poetic merits is either excluded or only treated in passing, for example by the taking up of a positive assessment of Clare's use of dialect:

> Verleugnet doch Clare auch in seinen Gedichten seinen landschaftlichen Dialekt und die Sprachweise des einfachen Landmanns nicht, und ich glaube, daß gerade dies seinen Werken einen so seltenen Reiz, einen so originellen Zauber verleiht.

> (Clare does not deny his regional dialect and the simple peasant's manner of speech in his poems, and I think that it is this which lends to his works their rare appeal, their original magic.)[20]

The anonymous German author reduces the complexity of Taylor's argument in his emphasis on the complexity of Clare's thought, for example, by focusing solely on the simplicity of his language. The moral overtones invoking a seemingly better life in the country are hard to miss.

Interestingly, the article in the *Literarisches Conversations-Blatt* from 1822 ends with a passage that does not draw upon Taylor's piece in the *London Magazine*. Here, the anonymous German author interprets Clare's current situation and predicts its development in the future. It is significant enough to warrant an extended quotation:

> Der Dichter scheint sich jedoch über Verdienste glücklich zu fühlen, und schlägt die kleinen Vortheile, die ihm die Herausgabe seiner Gedichtsammlung verschafft hat, sehr hoch an. Jedoch treibt er vor wie nach die Woche hindurch seine Handarbeit, besonders in den Gärten der benachbarten Landedelleute, und er ist zufrieden, seine Abende und Sonntage der Dichtkunst widmen zu können. Er scheint weit davon entfernt zu sein, eine Veränderung seiner jetzigen Lage zu wünschen; der Gedanke, seinen Geburtstort und seinen Stand zu verlassen, und ein gemächliches Leben in der Stadt zu führen, scheint ihm nie einzufallen. Sein Ruf als Dichter erfreut ihn, ohne ihn stolz zu machen, und seine Muse wird zur Dienerin seiner kindlichen Liebe, indem sie ihm die Pflege seines alten, verkrüppelten Vaters erleichtert.

> (The poet seems to be happy about his deserts and highly appreciates the small advantages procured by the publication of his collection of poems. Nonetheless, he continues his handiwork throughout the week, especially in the gardens of the neighbouring country gentlemen, and he is content to dedicate his evenings and Sundays to poetry. He seems far removed from wishing a change of his current condition; the thought of leaving his birthplace and his class does not seem to occur to him. He is delighted by his reputation as a poet without being proud of it, and his muse becomes the servant of his filial love by easing his care for his old, crippled father.)[21]

The writer's moralising impetus emerges most clearly in these concluding remarks. The image of the peasant content with his lot does not correspond to the reality of Clare's life, as revealed, for example, in his letters, where he repeatedly complains about the lack of acknowledgement both ideally and monetarily. Moreover, his often manic writing is no genteel occupation for 'evenings and Sundays', but is often situated on the spot in fields or during work. The German trend to reduce Clare to the moral cipher of the simple and content 'peasant poet' who had already appeared in the first article in the *Morgenblatt* has by now come to full bloom.

From that point on, German interest in Clare is sustained, albeit in a less prominent fashion. Evidence can be found in a short notice in the *Morgenblatt für gebildete Stände* from 17 August 1824. As part of the 'Literarische Notizen' ('Literary Notes'), it is mentioned that Clare is working on his 'New Shepherd's Calendar'.[22] The next reference to Clare is in the same magazine, on 12 May 1826. In a section entitled 'Berichte über die englische Literatur' ('Reports on English Literature') and after more extensive reviews of Percy Bysshe Shelley, Thomas Moore, Walter Scott, William Wordsworth, Robert Southey, Samuel Rogers and Thomas Campbell, Clare is mentioned in passing as someone who 'hat so manches zarte Lied gesungen, daß er hier genannt zu werden verdient' ('has sung many a tender song and thus deserves to be mentioned here').[23] *The Shepherd's Calendar* is mentioned, but is allotted the wrong year of publication (1825 instead of 1827).

Consolidation of interest – John Clare in German encyclopaedias
In 1827, the next significant German discussion of John Clare appears – this time not in a literary magazine, but in an important encyclopaedia. The *Allgemeine deutsche Real-Encyklopädie für die gebildeten Stände (Conversations-Lexikon)* is still published today and is best known by the name of its publisher, *Brockhaus*. The seventh edition of 1827 mentions Clare in its article 'Englische Poesie' ('English Poetry') as a 'Naturdichter' ('nature poet') alongside Hogg and confers on him the dubious status of a contemporary poet who has to be mentioned at least by name.[24] More significantly however, the encyclopaedia finally includes Clare's biography (the one announced five years earlier in the summary of Taylor's visit to Clare) in its seventh edition, the second edition published after Clare's appearance on the literary scene.[25] The focus and tone of this biographical entry form a direct and effective continuation of the article in the *Literarisches Conversations-Blatt* from 1822 by the same publisher. Clare's childhood is depicted as full of the 'Leiden der tiefen Armuth' ('sufferings of deep poverty'). The essay emphasises the way in which Clare worked hard to gain an education: 'und so gelang es John, sich durch Feierabendarbeit das Schulgeld zu ersparen, um lesen zu lernen' ('and in this way John was able to earn his tuition fee through after hour work, in order to learn reading').[26] The entry then faithfully traces Clare's life, starting with his reading

of *Robinson Crusoe* and then covering his first poetic inspiration through the reading of Thomson's *Seasons*, his education with John Turnill and his autodidactic playing of the fiddle up until the 'discovery' of his sonnet 'The Setting Sun' by Edward Drury (whose town is incorrectly called 'Hamford' instead of 'Stamford'), and then on to the publication of Clare's first volume of poetry. The resulting narrative is that of a simple and honest peasant boy bent on improving himself through dedication and hard work: 'Ohne Aufmunterung, nur zur eigenen Freude, dichtete Clare 13 Jahre lang, besang Gott und seine schöne Natur und arbeitete dabei mit Hacke und Spaten' ('Clare wrote poetry for 13 years without encouragement, purely for his own joy, extolling God and his beautiful nature and continued working with hoe and spade').[27] In this way, Clare is again subsumed into a moral narrative that often does not correspond with his actual life. Central to this narrative is the lack of aspiration ascribed to him: 'doch ist er seinem Dorfe und seinem Stande treu geblieben' ('yet he remained faithful to his village and his class'). The 'peasant poet' is a moral example only insofar as he does not question the social position society has given him. This interpretation of his life and poetry completely disregards his more revolutionary side, for example his criticism of enclosure or of upstart country squires. In fact, given the fact that Clare is included in the encyclopaedia as a poet, the biographical entry curiously sidelines his poetry, thereby continuing a trend already visible in the earlier magazine articles. The entry refers to four of his poems, 'The morning walk', 'The evening walk', The Setting Sun' and 'Address to Plenty, in Winter'. Among these, only the last one is discussed any further, and only to emphasise its 'herzzeißende [...] Wahrheit' ('heartbreaking truthfulness'[28]) – exactly the same sentimentalizing formulation that appears in the article in the *Literarisches Conversations-Blatt* from 1822. The overall assessment of Clare's poetry in the encyclopaedia's biographical entry remains lukewarm. The poems are

> einfach, ansprechend durch Wahrheit und Innigkeit, und voll origineller Bilder. Einige neue Wörter und Provinzialismen stören den Genuß derselben ein wenig, können aber, ohne ihre Eigenthümlichkeit anzutasten, nicht getilgt werden.

> (simple, appealing through their truthfulness and intimacy, and full of original images. Some new words and provincialisms disturb their enjoyment a little, but cannot be deleted without infringing on their idiosyncrasy.)[29]

The 'original magic' of Clare's dialect words that the author in the 1822 *Literarisches Conversations-Blatt* praised seems to have disappeared in the perception of the German critics in 1827. The eighth and ninth editions of the *Allgemeine deutsche Real-Encyklopädie* (1833 and 1843 respectively) retain this article mostly unchanged. The article in the new *Meyers Konversationslexikon* (edition '0', 1840-52) is – with the exception of some differences in phrasing –an exact copy of the earlier one, right down to the wrong name of Drury's hometown.[30]

The moral of Clare's madness

By the time of the next significant publication on Clare in Germany in 1840, the poet's life had changed significantly. By now, his final volume, *The Rural Muse* (1835), had been published, Clare had moved to a new cottage in Northborough in 1832 and had been admitted to the asylum in Epping Forest in 1837. The fact that across all of this time, Clare was not being discussed in German publications demonstrates that the development of his literary success (or his lack thereof) in this country closely corresponds to his reception in England. Perhaps not surprisingly, it is Clare's madness that gives new life to German interest in him perhaps because of the opportunity it afforded to continue and deepen the already established moralising narrative for which he had become a bearer. On 27 August 1840, the *Blätter für literarische Unterhaltung* ('Pages for Literary Entertainment') published an article with the headline 'Der Dichter Clare, ein Opfer seiner literarischen Gönner' ('The poet Clare, a victim of his literary benefactors').[31] This article was probably inspired by rumours circulated in the British press that Clare had died.[32] The introduction reads as follows:

Der unseligen und unverantwortlichen, vorzüglich in England herrschenden Manie, welche der Brite zu euphemistisch mit dem Namen des System of lionizing bezeichnet, die aber in nichts Geringerem besteht, als in der verwerflichen Sucht, womit Menschen, die zu einer Erhebung und Auszeichnung durch eigene Kraft unfähig sind, ihrer Eitelkeit durch eine Curiositätenkrämerei schmeicheln, welcher Nichts, selbst der Mensch und das Talent nicht, zu gering sind, um zur Befriedigung ihres Gelüstes zu dienen – diese Manie, welche glücklicherweise seit einigen Jahren in jenem Lande einigermaßen nachgelassen hat, ist in der neuesten Zeit ein neues Opfer gefallen – der Dichter Clare.

(The unfortunate and irresponsible mania, which is mostly prevalent in England and which the Briton too euphemistically calls by the name of the system of lionizing, but which consists in nothing less than in the condemnable addiction in which people incapable of elevation and honour by their own efforts flatter their vanity through dabbling with oddities in which nothing, not even the human being and talent are slight enough in order to serve for the satisfaction of their cravings; this mania, which fortunately has slackened more or less in that country for several years, has recently found a new victim – the poet Clare.)[33]

Moralising on the basis of class is here joined by a new nationalist tone which suggests that a dangerous dissolution of class boundaries is a specifically English trend – one whose victim Clare has become. The author then goes on the explain the particular nature of Clare's victimhood. He criticises a patronage

welche auf Naturdichter und Bauernpoeten Jagd macht, Leute, die an den Erwerb ihres nöthigsten Unterhalts gewöhnt sind, aus dem Kreise ihrer täglichen Beschäftigung herausreißt und dann, wenn ihre eigene Eitelkeit befriedigt und der Reiz der Neuheit vorüber ist, sie mit einer in ihnen bewirkten Aufregung ihrer Gefühle und einer unnatürlichen Verfeinerung ihres ursprünglich einfachen Geschmacks beschenkt, wieder in die harte Lage ihres vormaligen Looses zurücksinken läßt.

(which hunts nature poets and peasant poets, people who are used to earning their basic livelihood, takes them out of the circle of their daily occupation and when their own vanity is satisfied and the allure of the novelty is over, lets them sink back into the tough conditions of their former destiny, but now with an excitement of the emotions caused in them and presented with an unnatural refinement of their formerly simple tastes.)[34]

It is noticeable that the author does not deem the poetry of these 'nature and peasant poets' worthy of attention in the first place, but clearly sees them only as a fashionable craze. The poetic output enabled by even a short or insufficient patronage is in his eyes not enough to justify the unsettling of the peasant poets' class consciousness. Tellingly, the 'excitement of the emotions' and the 'refinement of [...] tastes' is not something that made these writers poets in the first place – it is an 'unnatural' addition only caused by undue attention.

Clare's madness serves him as a proof for this theory, since the poet entered into it 'unter seinen convulsischen, abgerissenen und deshalb unproductiven Anstrengungen' ('under convulsive, incoherent and therefore unproductive efforts').[35] In the light of this appraisal, it is not surprising that the article contains no actual quotations of Clare's poetry. The author of the article then paraphrases an appeal published by Dr Matthew Allen, physician and founder of the asylum where Clare was living at that time, in the *Times*, in which Allen suggests a yearly stipend in order to settle Clare's mind.[36] He wants to achieve this by publishing a new volume of Clare's poems, whose intrinsic value the German author immediately lowers by describing it as of 'mindestens von psychologischem Interesse' ('at least of psychological interest').[37] Allen's appeal is therefore subsumed into a condescending pseudo-philanthropic gesture by the author of the German article, which aims not at the defence of Clare's poetic reputation but at the establishment of him as a moral parable: the 'lost soul' to be pitied.

Clare's change of fortune also leads to an addition to his biographical entry in the tenth edition of *Allgemeine Deutsche Real-Encyklopädie* in 1852.[38] Again, he is depicted as a victim, this time in a failed land-speculation scheme:

Zum Unglück ließ er sich jedoch verleiten, in Land zu speculieren, verlor hierbei seine ganze Habe und versank, seinem Mißgeschick erliegend, in düstere Schwermuth, sodaß er nach einer Irrenanstalt gebracht werden mußte.

(Unfortunately, he was fooled into speculating with land, lost all his property and, succumbing to his ill fortune, sunk into gloomy melancholy so that he had to be brought to a mental asylum.)[39]

The basic narrative is the same that we have seen in previous accounts: the simple peasant is misguided by others, leaves his familiar surroundings, reaches beyond his station and is punished for this by madness. This is a more obvious construction because the purported reason – the failed land speculation – has no basis in Clare's reality. In a condescending manner similar to earlier representations of Clare, the article in the encyclopaedia explicitly selects his later poetry for recommendation for its 'gewähltere und correctere Diction' ('more refined and correct diction') – i.e. for its greater conformity.[40] Moreover, his wife Patty is referred to as 'die Geliebte seiner Jugend' ('the love of his youth'), thereby skilfully suppressing the improper presence of the actual 'love of his youth', Mary Joyce, and along with her a more sexual side of Clare's character – existing beyond the neat confines of marriage – which might have threatened to unsettle the established moral narrative.[41] This biographical entry becomes the basis for further editions, both of the *Allgemeine deutsche Real-Encyklopädie* and of the *Meyers Konversationslexikon*. The eleventh edition only adds the date of Clare's death. Later editions of both encyclopaedias increasingly condense the biographical entry for Clare, but continue to include him.[42]

A turn to the poetry: Clare's first anthology appearance

As we have seen, the actual poetry written by Clare is not given much room in German publications. Occasional lines are quoted, titles are referred to, but across the texts considered so far, none quotes an entire poem. This changed in 1852 with the third expanded edition of Oskar Ludwig Bernhard Wolff's[43] anthology *Hausschatz englischer Poesie* ('Home Treasure of English Poetry').[44] Earlier editions did not include Clare, and his inclusion by the volume's editor Heinrich August Manitius[45], who took over after Wolff's death, as part of the 'sehr vermehrte und verbesserte Auflage' ('greatly increased and improved edition')[46] was noted explicitly in the review published in 1852 in the magazine *Die Grenzboten, Zeitschrift für Politik, Literatur und Kunst* ('The Border Heralds, Newspaper for Politics, Literature and Art').[47] The anthology encompassed English poetry 'von Chaucer bis auf die neueste Zeit' ('from Chaucer until the most recent time'). Manitius' new entry on Clare includes a short biographical sketch and six complete poems in the original English: 'What is Life?',[48] 'Summer Morning', 'The Primrose – A Sonnet', 'The Thrush's Nest – A Sonnet', 'Dawnings of Genius' and 'A Sonnet to the Glow-worm'. Manitius does not provide translations of these poems. For the first time, the German reader without access to the original English publications can discover the nature poetry for which Clare has been praised: five out of the six poems belong to this category. 'Dawnings of a Genius' in particular can be seen as autobiographical when read in the context of the biography given by Manitius. Even though he repeats the story about Clare's failed lease speculations as the reason for his 'Schwermuth' ('melancholia'), Manitius does not paint him as a madman.[49] In fact, he does not mention that Clare was still resident in an asylum but states rather vaguely that 'vor einigen Jahren lebte er noch' ('some years ago he was still alive'), as if there were no current news available about Clare.[50]

He refers to the first two volumes of poetry by Clare but not to *The Shepherd's Calendar* or *The Rural Muse*. Instead, he incorrectly lists the pamphlet Clare wrote in 1818 as an advertisement for a volume of his poetry that the printer Henson had promised to publish, 'A Collection of Original Trifles', as Clare's first publication to which he also ascribes the wrong date (1817). Yet more important than these minor factual mistakes is Manitius' positive assessment of Clare's poetry. For him, 'Clare's Glück ging indess schnell vorüber, während ihm sein Dichterruf für alle Zeiten bleiben wird' ('Clare's luck was soon over, whereas he will retain his reputation as a poet for all times').[51] Manitius also gives the first description of Clare's poetic method in German: 'Seine Dichtungen sind der unmittelbare Erguss inniger Empfindungen, wie sie auf Fluren und Spaziergängen in ihm hervorgerufen wurden' ('His poetry is the immediate effusion of intimate emotions as brought about by open fields and on walks').[52]

In the year that Clare died, a second anthology that included his work is published, Hermann Simon's *Auswahl englischer Gedichte. Aus dem Englischen ins Deutsche übertragen* (1864) ('Selection of English Poems. Translated from English into German'). His biographical information, relegated to the index, is only three sentences long and also, like others before it, establishes a clear link between speculation, poverty and madness: 'In Folge unglücklicher Speculationen ganz verarmt, wurde er schwermüthig und starb in einer Irrenanstalt' ('As the result of unhappy speculations completely impoverished, he became melancholic and died in a mental asylum').[53] The inclusion of 'What is life'[54] as the only poem reinforces the image created of the poet. Importantly though, Simon provides the first verse translation of Clare into German. He transfers the original rhyme scheme competently and precisely into German. More importantly however, he is able to condense the language of his translation in order to achieve an imitation of the brevity and clarity of English that translations into German often lack. Sometimes, nuances of meaning have to be sacrificed to Simon's two stylistic main principles, for example when he translates 'A cobweb, hiding disappointment's thorn' as 'Ein Spinngewebe, bergend der Täuschung stechend Licht' (literally: 'A cobweb, hiding the piercing light of deception') in order to create a rhyme.[55] The resulting image is not very felicitous as it is surely odd to have deception positioned as 'piercing light' – light being more often associated with the clarifying reason of Enlightenment. In his translation of the line 'And peace? Where can it's happiness abound?', Herman has to lose the reference to happiness in order not to create too long a sentence: 'Und was ist Fricden? Sag, wer jemals ihn wohl fand?' (literally: 'And what is peace? Tell me, who could ever find it?').[56] Yet the translation of the final stanza shows Hermann's skill as a translator at its fullest (even though a rhyme by simply using the same 'ist' construction is rather weak):

> 'Tis but a trial all must undergo;
> To teach unthankful mortals how to prize
> That happiness vain man's denied to know,
> Until he's call'd to claim it in the skies.

> Nur eine Prüfung ist's, die Alle tragen müssen,
> Sie lehrt dem Undank, wie so herrlich ist
> Die Seligkeit, die Hochmuth wird vermissen
> Bis einst der Geist verklärt im Himmel ist.

Hermann is able to condense 'unthankful mortal' and 'vain man's' into the two personified abstractions 'Undank' and 'Hochmuth', thereby maintaining the impetus of the poem.

The *Hausschatz englischer Poesie* and *Auswahl englischer Gedichte* and the already-mentioned *Briefe an eine deutsche Edelfrau über die neuesten englischen Dichter* seem to be the only German anthologies of the nineteenth century that include Clare. He is not present in the two well-known anthologies by Ferdinand Freiligrath, *Englische Gedichte aus neuerer Zeit. Nach Felicia Hermans, Robert Southey, Alfred Tennyson, Henry W. Longfellow und Andren* (1846) or *The Rose, Thistle and Shamrock. A Selection of English Poetry, Chiefly Modern* (1853), the latter of which was 'the most successful anthology or English lyrical poetry in nineteenth-century Germany'.[57] Clare was also not represented in Ludwig Herrig's influential anthology *The British Classical Authors. Select Specimens of the National Literature of England from G. Chaucer to the Present Time. Poetry and Prose* (1850), which however does include another labouring-class poet – James Hogg. Nor was he part of Heinrich Stadelmann's *Leierklänge aus Albion. Eine Auswahl englischer Gedichte in's Deutsche übertragen* (1864), even though it had a separate category for 'Natur und Menschenleben' ('nature and human life').

Clare's death

After Hermann's anthology, German publications remain relatively quiet on Clare until his death in 1864.[58] This occasion prompts two longer biographical articles in the *same* magazine, the *Magazin für die Literatur des Auslandes*, one on 18 February and the other on 7 October 1865. The first article bears the title 'Der Bauernpoet John Clare' ('The peasant poet John Clare').[59] The London-based magazine *The Bookseller* is given as the source of the news about Clare's death. The German article provides the longest biography of Clare yet available in German. The tone is more detailed and narrative than in earlier biographical sketches, for example in a detailed description of how Clare first encountered Thomson's *Seasons* and read it in Burghley Park. For the first time, Clare's relative physical weakness is mentioned ('ein armseliges, gebrechliches, schwächliches Kind' ('a destitute, frail and feeble child').[60] The author also describes the origin of Clare's pamphlet 'Address to the Public', but without mentioning Henson.[61] Even though the general tone resembles Manitius' short biographical sketch in its positive assessment more than that of earlier publications, a continuing tendency to moralise on Clare's social status and his destiny remains. Again, no mention is made of Mary Joyce, and the whole force of love that propelled his poetry is attributed to Martha Turner. The anonymous German author notes approvingly that Clare never forgot that it was a bookseller who helped in his 'Erhebung aus dem Dunkel und äußerster Bedrängnis' ('elevation from darkness and utmost hardship') and that he lacked the 'Selbstüberschätzung' ('hubris') of other writers in similar situations.[62] The article, like the others before it, also emphasises Clare's hard work for his education. For example, the German author claims that Clare 'arbeitete [...] wie ein Sklave' ('worked like a slave') in order to earn the money to buy his copy of *The Seasons*.[63] Yet in fact, Clare got the money from his father.[64] And finally, the reason for his decline into madness is given as 'eine ganze Herde von neugierigen Reisenden' ('a whole flock of nosy travellers') which 'rief ihn ab von seinen Garten-Beschäftigungen, zog ihn in's Wirtshaus, um sentimentalen Unsinn zu schwatzen und natürlich "ein Glas zu trinken"' ('called him away from his employment in the garden, dragged him into the pub in order to babble sentimental nonsense and of course to "have a drink"').[65]

Yet the positive review of Clare and particularly of his poetry in this article is more important than these links to a moralising strain of interpretation. The German author quotes a longer passage from a review in *The Quarterly Review*, that 'große kritische Organ' ('great institution of criticism') as evidence for Clare's greatness – 'acht

Seiten höchst vortheilhafter Besprechung' ('a most advantageous review of eight pages') cannot lie![66] In his introduction, the German author claims that Clare's importance in England is immense: He is the one 'den die Engländer anzuführen pflegen, wenn man ihnen vorwirft, daß sie eine Nation von Shopkeepers sind und Sinn und Verständnis für ungesuchte, natürliche Poesie verloren haben' ('who the English invoke when they are accused of being a nation of shopkeepers who have lost the sense and understanding for an unforced, natural poetry').[67] He then compares Clare with the 'niedersächsischen Bauernpoeten Heinrich Janßen' ('Heinrich Janßen [actually: Hinrich Janssen, 1697-1737], the peasant poet from Lower Saxony'). Clare is declared the greater of the two, since he 'übertrifft ihn [...] an Schwung der Verse und Tiefe des Gedankens. Sein Genie ist unmittelbarer, mit idealerem Zuge und hat wohl deshalb auch sein Leben so romantisch unglücklich gestaltet' ('surpasses him in the momentum of his verse and the depths of his thoughts. His [Clare's] genius is more immediate, with a more idealistic streak, and therefore has probably shaped his life so romantically unhappy').[68] For the author of the German article, Clare's poetic genius is intrinsically bound up with his madness.

In his conclusion, the German author claims for Clare the epithet Carlyle intended for Robert Burns: 'ein Riese der Ursprünglichkeit, einer jener Menschen, welche niederreichen bis zu den ewigen Tiefen und mit den Heroen unseres Geschlechts ihren Rang einnehmen' ('a giant Original Man; one of those men who reach down to the perennial Deeps, who take rank with the Heroic among men').[69] High praise indeed! For the German author, the strongest evidence for this can be found in Clare's last volume, *The Rural Muse*, which contains 'Stücke, die dem Besten, was jemals in englischen Versen geschrieben wurde, nach dem Urtheile genauer und gründlicher Kenner in England selbst, gleichkommt' ('pieces which rival the best that was ever written in English verse, according to the judgment of accurate and thorough experts in England itself').[70] He is therefore looking forward to a forthcoming edition of Clare's hitherto unpublished poems from his time in the asylum. The author finishes with an appeal to translate Clare into German, since 'deutsche Übersetzungen des englischen Bauernpoeten sind uns nicht bekannt geworden' ('German translations of the English peasant poet are not known to us').[71] As we have seen, this statement is not entirely correct, but one prose and one verse translation during Clare's lifetime is not much, so the author's appeal remains valid. Unfortunately, its fulfilment would have to wait for more than a hundred years, when Georg von der Vring includes translations of 'Clock a Clay' and 'I hid my love when young' in his anthology *English Horn* in 1953.[72]

The second article in the *Magazin für die Literatur des Auslandes* on Clare's death also marks the endpoint of his German reception in the nineteenth century. Published on 7 October 1865, it is entitled 'Ein Dichterleben' ('A poet's life') and occasioned by the publication of Frederick Martin's biography.[73] The German author closely follows Martin in terms of content and in particular in 'the colourful narrative embroidery that Martin always added'.[74] The poverty of Clare's upbringing is stressed even more than in earlier biographical sketches. Clare is described as being born 'in der traurigsten Gegend Englands, [...] in der traurigsten Lehmhütte' ('in the saddest region of England, [...] the saddest mud hut') to the 'ärmsten, verwahrlosten Aeltern' ('poorest, unkempt parents').[75] He is surrounded by 'einer nebeligen Ebene voller Sümpfe und stagnirenden Pfützen' ('a foggy plain full of swamps and stagnant puddles') and his special skill lay in his ability to turn such dismal surroundings into poetry.[76]

In addition to the already published events in Clare's life, the German author describes some new scenes for the first time. He mentions Clare's twin who died at birth. He narrates Clare's walk to the 'Gränzlinie des Horizonts' ('edge of the orison') and turns this phrase into a metaphor for a poetic sensibility which strives, like young Clare, 'die Stelle zu erreichen, wo sich Himmel und Erde berühren' ('to reach the spot where heaven and earth touch').[77] He also recounts Clare's work as a potboy in the Blue Bell and provides a more accurate though imperfect account of the source of the money Clare used to buy *The Seasons* ('Der Vater hatte keinen Schilling übrig, aber die gute Mutter brachte mit vieler Mühe wenigstens sieben Pence zusammen, und die fehlenden fünf wurden von verschiedenen Stammgästen der 'blauen Glocke' als große Anleihe erhoben' ('The father could not spare a shilling, but his good mother could muster with difficultly seven pence, and the missing five were raised as a great loan from various regulars of the 'Blue Bell'').[78] For the first time, the poet's first love Mary is mentioned (though her surname is incorrectly given as 'Joyor') and described as the 'ideale Jugendliebe' ('ideal love of his youth').[79] Clare's mother's destruction of the scraps of paper on which Clare wrote his poetry is described not as the accident that it actually was, but as purposeful and malignant, since 'die Poesie gehörte nicht dahin, störte nur die Arbeit' ('the poetry did not belong there but only interfered with his chores').[80] Clare's time as a soldier and his stay with the local gipsies is also mentioned and seen as a source of poetic inspiration.[81] The German author also briefly recounts Clare's escape from the asylum in order to go back to Mary.[82]

Yet it is the more colourful details of Clare's life to which the German author returns again and again. A central passage towards the end describes how Clare's physical and mental health was allegedly destroyed by the hard physical labour to which he had to return after 'Clare's Dichtungen von Feldern und Blumen mit dem frischen Thau darauf waren nicht mehr Mode' ('Clare's poems of fields and flowers with fresh dew on them were no longer fashionable').[83] The choice of words discloses the German author's own disdain for a poetry that is perceived as merely dainty or decorative.[84] Clare's publisher is depicted as being co-responsible for his madness: 'Er schreib herzzerreißend an seinen Verleger in London. Keine Antwort. Dieser hatte ein gutes Geschäft mit ihm gemacht und Honorar war ja nicht ausgemacht worden.' ('He wrote piteously to his publisher in London. No reply. The publisher had made a good bargain with him and no fee had been agreed upon').[85] Unusually, the article quotes a complete poem 'I am' in the original English, yet does so not in order to analyse its poetic merits but to use it as proof for the proffered moral narrative of Clare as one who suffered his ordained fate 'ruhig, aber mit stillem Kummer' ('calmly, but with quiet sorrow').[86] The last lines of the poem especially – 'untroubled where I lie / The grass below—above the vaulted sky' – are taken as a prolepsis of Clare's imminent death.[87] The closing remarks also introduce a nationalist criticism of England's treatment of Clare: 'einem der holdesten Sänger der Natur, der je geboren ward innerhalb des lieben alten England, des lieben alten England, das so stolz ist auf seine Milchstraße edler Dichter und so verwüsterisch mit deren Leben' ('one of the fairest poets of nature who was born in good old England, that good old England that is so proud of its Milky Way of noble poets and so devastating to their lives').[88] Unlike the previous article dealing with Clare and his poetry, this final piece published on him in Germany in the nineteenth century unfortunately returns to the moralising narrative dominant in earlier articles, trying to turn Clare's life into a 'memento mori' without any real regard for his poetry. After this article from 7 October 1865, Clare's reception in Germany breaks off for over 100 years.[89] Clare's death seems to have put a final stop to a reception that was interested more in his life than in his poetry. The scarcity of translated poems and the lack of a larger interested in

Clare's own country means that there a lack of input that could have continued or increased the momentum of his reception in Germany.

NOTES

1   Horst Oppel, *Englisch-deutsche Literaturbeziehungen. II. Von der Romantik bis zur Gegenwart* (Berlin: Erich Schmidt Verlag, 1971), p. 40.

2   Thomas Finkenstaedt, *Kleine Geschichte der Anglistik in Deutschland. Eine Einführung* (Darmstadt: Wissenschaftliche Buchgesellschaft, 1983), p. 36 ff.

3   Horst Oppel, pp. 35 ff.

4   'The journal had a circulation of 2,500 copies, 1,400 of which were subscriptions. [...] [I]ts scope ranged from literature and art, travel reports to articles about topics concerned with natural sciences.' Cf. Torsten Caeners, 'Tennyson's Reception in Germany', in *The Reception of Alfred Tennyson in Europe*, ed. by Leonée Ormond (London: Bloomsbury Academic, 2016), pp. 193-230 (p. 193).

5   Cf. *Quarterly Review*, May 1820, pp. 166-174; and Jonathan Bate, *Biography*, p. 156.

6   This and the following translations are my own.

7   *Quarterly Review*, May 1820, p. 173.

8   *Das Morgenblatt für gebildete Stände*, Literatur-Blatt Nr. 87, 20 October 1820, pp. 346 ff.

9   Not surprisingly, it is the picture of Lord Byron that opens the volume.

10   Friedrich Johann Jacobsen, *Briefe an eine deutsche Edelfrau über die neusten englischen Dichter, herausgegeben mit übersetzten Auszügen vorzüglicher Stellen aus ihren Gedichten und mit den Bildnissen der berühmtesten jetzt lebenden Dichter Englands* (Hamburg Altona: J. F. Hammerich, 1820), p. 733.

11   Published by Brockhaus between 1920 and 1926. The publisher was (and still is) mainly renowned for its encyclopaedia.

12   *Beilage zum literarischen Conversations-Blatt*, 28 February 1821, p. 201.

13   *Literarisches Conversations-Blatt*, No 54, 5 March 1822, pp. 215 ff.

14   *London Magazine*, November 1821, pp. 540-48.

15   *Literarisches Conversations-Blatt*, 5 March 1822, p. 215.

16   I will discuss Clare's first biography in German and its evolvement through later editions of the encyclopaedia later on in this article.

17   *London Magazine*, November 1821, pp. 540-44.

18   *Literarisches Conversations-Blatt*, 5 March 1822, p. 215.

19   Ibid., p. 216

20   Ibid.

21   Ibid.

22   *Das Morgenblatt für gebildete Stände*, Literatur-Blatt Nr. 66, 17 August 1824, p. 265.

23   *Das Morgenblatt für gebildete Stände*, Literatur-Blatt Nr. 38, 12 May 1824, p. 151.

24   *Allgemeine deutsche Real-Encyklopädie für die gebildeten Stände (Conversations-Lexikon)*, 7th edn., vol. 3 D-E, 1827 (Leipzig: Brockhaus, 1827), p. 581.

25   The previous, sixth edition was published in 1824.

26   Ibid., p. 701.

27 Ibid.

28 Ibid.

29 Ibid.

30 *Meyers Konversationslexikon*, edition '0', volume 7, 2nd part, Charpentier – Conomorpha (Hildburghausen, Amsterdam, Paris and Philadelphia: Druck und Verlag des Bibliographischen Instituts, 1845), pp. 796 ff.

31 *Blätter für literarische Unterhaltung*, 27 August 1840, p. 969.

32 Cf. Simon Kövesi, 'John Clare's deaths: poverty, education and poetry', in *New Essay on John Clare. Poetry, Culture and Community*, ed. by Simon Kövesi and Scott McEathron (Cambridge: Cambridge University Press, 2015), p. 153.

33 Ibid.

34 Ibid.

35 Ibid.

36 Before this, the German author has already referred to Dr Allen in his deconstruction of the myth of Clare's death as it has been wrongly reported by the *Halifax Express*.

37 Ibid.

38 There were only to other references to Clare between 1840 and 1852: *Morgenblatt für gebildete Leser* printed some lines in the original English from his poems 'What is life' and 'Our own fireside' as a sort of introductory motto for the day on 26 February 26 and 14 June, 1845, respectively (cf. *Morgenblatt für gebildete Leser*, p. 193 and p. 565). Both excerpts reflect on vanity and thus perfectly fit into the moralising narrative established around Clare in 19th century Germany.

39 *Allgemeine deutsche Real-Encyklopädie für die gebildeten Stände (Conversations-Lexikon)*, 10th edn., vol. 4, Cevennen – Deutschland (Leipzig: Brockhaus, 1852), p. 225.

40 Ibid.

41 Ibid.

42 Cf. for example the 17th edition of the *Brockhaus Enzyklopädie*, Volume 4, 1968.

43 Oskar Ludwig Bernhard Wolff (1799-1851), German-Jewish writer, humourist and pedagogue, in contact with Goethe, Marx, Heine, Liszt and Wagner and translated from English, French, Italian, Spanish, Latin and Greek.

44 O. L. B.Wolff, *Hausschatz englischer Poesie*, third edition, edited by H.A. Manitius (Leipzig: Hermann Costenoble, 1852), pp. 366-8.

45 Heinrich August Manitius (1804-83), teacher and private scholar.

46 O. L. B. Wolff, pp. 366-8.

47 *Die Grenzboten, Zeitschrift für Politik*, November 1852, p. 238.

48 Though without the stanza beginning 'And thou, O Trouble?' – possibly because the editor relied on a source different from *Poems Descriptive*.

49 O. L. B. Wolff, p. 366.

50 Ibid.

51 Ibid.

52 Ibid.

53 Hermann Simon, *Auswahl englischer Gedichte. Aus dem Englischen ins Deutsche übertragen* (Leipzig: Arnoldische Buchhandlung, 1864), p. 361.

54 As in Wolff's anthology, without the stanza beginning 'And thou, O Trouble?'

55 Ibid., p. 145.

56   Ibid.

57   Torsten Caeners, p. 200.

58   The only exception is a passing reference in the *Magazin für die Literatur des Auslandes* (*Magazine for Foreign Literature*) on 30 April 1859, as part of an article that severely criticizes contemporary English literature. Yet it acknowledges that the 'poetische Bauer Clare' ('the poetic peasant Clare') writes about love 'nicht traurig und sentimental, sondern mit leidlichem Humor' ('not sadly and sentimentally, but tolerably humorously'). (Cf. *Magazin für die Literatur des Auslandes*, 30 April 1859, p. 198.)

59   *Magazin für die Literatur des Auslandes*, 18 February 1865, pp. 107-9.

60   Ibid., p. 107.

61   Ibid., p. 108.

62   Ibid.

63   Ibid., p. 107.

64   Cf. Bate, *Biography*, p. 90.

65   *Magazin für die Literatur des Auslandes*, 18 February 1865, p. 108.

66   Ibid.

67   Ibid., p. 107.

68   Ibid.

69   Ibid., p. 108.

70   Ibid.

71   Ibid., p. 109.

72   Georg von der Vring, *Englisch Horn. Anthologie angelsächsischer Lyrik von den Anfängen bis zur Gegenwart* (Köln and Berlin: Kiepenheuer & Witsch, 1953), pp. 101 ff.

73   *Magazin für die Literatur des Auslandes*, 7 October 1865, pp. 569-71.

74   Bate, *Biography*, p. 10.

75   *Magazin für die Literatur des Auslandes*, 7 October 1865, p. 569.

76   Ibid.

77   Ibid.

78   Ibid.

79   Ibid.

80   Ibid., p. 570.

81   Ibid.

82   Ibid., p. 571.

83   Ibid.

84   It is telling that the author does not seem to be aware of *The Rural Muse* (he calls *The Shepherd's Calendar* 'seine letzte poetische Anstrengung' ('his last poetical effort'), which was described as Clare's strongest volume of poetry in the same magazine only eight months earlier).

85   Ibid.

86   Ibid. The version of 'I am' included in the German article differs on several accounts from the poem as printed in *John Clare*, ed. by Eric Robinson and David Powell (Oxford: Oxford University Press, 1984), p. 361.

87   Ibid.

88   Ibid.

89   The rare interactions with Clare in the twentieth century and the more thorough revival of interest and revaluation of his poetry in the twenty-first century will be the focus of my second essay on this topic.

An Index of Significant Publications on John Clare, 2019-2020

Andrew Hodgson and Erin Lafford

This annual index of new significant publications on John Clare accounts for the year 2019-2020, and also includes any publications overlooked in previous indexes running from 2011-2019. This index has four categories: books, chapters in books and edited collections, articles, and other publications and projects. As the date for each entry is provided in its citation, we do not divide the index into yearly sections, but offer instead a bibliography for each category that collects material published between 2019-20. All of the publications indexed have been selected for either their sole or significant focus on Clare's works, and so we have not included publications which, whilst of interest regarding the wider field of Romantic studies, do not make substantial reference to Clare. We have strived for as much coverage as possible, but there will inevitably be some omissions and we welcome correspondence from anybody who has suggestions about overlooked publications that can be added into subsequent indexes. Please email any suggestions to: e.lafford@derby.ac.uk or andrew.hodgson@bham.ac.uk.

Books
Kövesi, Simon, ed., *The Meeting: Reading and Writing Through John Clare* (Helpston: The John Clare Society, 2020).
— and Erin Lafford, eds., *Palgrave Advances in John Clare Studies* (London: Palgrave Macmillan, 2020).

Chapters in books and edited collections
Anderson, David, 'Crosses, Circles, and Madness: Iain Sinclair's *Lights Out for the Territory, London Orbital*, and *Edge of the Orison*', in *Landscape and Subjectivity in the Work of Patrick Keiller, W. G. Sebald, and Iain Sinclair* (Oxford: Oxford University Press, 2020), pp. 225-68.
Bushell, Sally, 'Unmapping John Clare: Circularity, Linearity, Temporality', in *Romantic Cartographies: Mapping, Literature, Culture, 1789-1832*, ed. by Damian Walford Davies, Julia S. Carlson, and Sally Bushell (Cambridge: Cambridge University Press, 2020), pp. 232-51.

Castell, James, 'John Clare's Dynamic Animals', in *Palgrave Advances in John Clare Studies*, ed. by Simon Kövesi and Erin Lafford (London: Palgrave Macmillan, 2020), pp. 157-177.

Castellano, Katey, 'Multispecies Work in John Clare's "Birds Nesting" Poems', in *Palgrave Advances in John Clare Studies*, ed. by Simon Kövesi and Erin Lafford (London: Palgrave Macmillan, 2020), pp. 179-197.

Derbyshire, Nancy M., 'The Labouring Class Bird', in *Birds in Eighteenth-Century Literature: Reason, Emotion, and Ornithology, 1700–1840*, ed. by Brycchan Carey, Sayre Greenfield, and Anne Milne (London: Palgrave Macmillan, 2020), pp. 99-110.

Dessau, Lily, 'Contracting Time: John Clare's *Shepherd's Calendar*', in *Romanticism and Time: Literary Temporalities*, ed. by Sophie Laniel-Musitelli and Céline Sabiron (Cambridge: Open Book, 2020), pp. 121-44.

Dodd, Elizabeth S., 'John Clare's Romantic 'I': A Prophetic Poetics of Testimony', in *Prophetic Witness and the Reimagining of the World: Poetry, Theology and Philosophy in Dialogue*, ed. by Mark S. Burrows, Hilary Davies, and Josephine von Zitzewitz (London: Routledge, 2020), pp. 136-47.

Harris, Alexandra, 'Moving House', in *Lives of Houses*, ed. by Kate Kennedy and Hermione Lee (Princeton; Oxford: Princeton University Press, 2020), pp. 3-17.

Hess, Scott, 'Biosemiosis and Posthumanism in John Clare's Multi-Centred Environments', in *Palgrave Advances in John Clare Studies*, ed. by Simon Kövesi and Erin Lafford (London: Palgrave Macmillan, 2020), pp. 199-219.

Hodgson, Andrew, 'Clare's Late Styles', in *The Lost Romantics: Forgotten Poets, Neglected Works, and One-Hit Wonders*, ed. by Norbert Lennartz (London: Palgrave Macmillan, 2020), pp. 151-68.

— 'John Clare's Ear: Metres and Rhythms', in *Palgrave Advances in John Clare Studies*, ed. by Simon Kövesi and Erin Lafford (London: Palgrave Macmillan, 2020), pp. 111-35.

Houghton-Walker, Sarah, 'John Clare's *The Shepherd's Calendar* and Forms of Repetition', in *Palgrave Advances in John Clare Studies*, ed. by Simon Kövesi and Erin Lafford (London: Palgrave Macmillan, 2020), pp. 137-56.

Lafford, Erin, '"fancys or feelings": John Clare's Hypochondriac Poetics', in *Palgrave Advances in John Clare Studies*, ed. by Simon Kövesi and Erin Lafford (London: Palgrave Macmillan, 2020), pp. 249-73.

Lodge, Sara, 'John Clare's Landforms', in *Palgrave Advances in John Clare Studies*, ed. by Simon Kövesi and Erin Lafford (London: Palgrave Macmillan, 2020), pp. 87-109.

McAlpine, Erica, 'Wondering about John Clare', in *The Poet's Mistake* (Princeton, NJ: Princeton University Press, 2020), pp. 74-89.

McCue, Kirsteen, '"Sweet the Merry Bells Ring Round": John Clare's Songs for the Drawing Room', in *Palgrave Advances in John Clare Studies*, ed. by Simon Kövesi and Erin Lafford (London: Palgrave Macmillan, 2020), pp. 37-60.

Nicholson, Michael, 'Common Distress: John Clare's Poetic Strain', in *Palgrave Advances in John Clare Studies*, ed. by Simon Kövesi and Erin Lafford (London: Palgrave Macmillan, 2020), pp. 221-47.

Phillips, Catherine, 'Hopkins and the Lost Beloved: The Making of "A Voice from the World" and "Binsey Poplars"', in *Poetry in the Making: Creativity and Composition in Victorian Poetic Drafts*, ed. by Daniel Tyler (Oxford: Oxford University Press, 2020), pp. 167-88.

Stewart, David, 'Poetry's Variety: John Clare and the Poetic Scene in the 1820s and 1830s', in *Palgrave Advances in John Clare Studies*, ed. by Simon Kövesi and Erin Lafford (London: Palgrave Macmillan, 2020), pp. 17-36.

Weiner, Stephanie Kuduk, '"Sea Songs Love Ballads &c &c": John Clare and Vernacular Song', in *Palgrave Advances in John Clare Studies*, ed. by Simon Kövesi and Erin Lafford (London: Palgrave Macmillan, 2020), pp. 61-85.

Whitehead, James, '"A Song in the Night": Reconsidering John Clare's Later Asylum Poetry', in *Palgrave Advances in John Clare Studies*, ed. by Simon Kövesi and Erin Lafford (London: Palgrave Macmillan, 2020), pp. 275-96.

Articles

Brooks, Martin, 'Edward Thomas and the Imagination', *English Literature in Transition, 1880-1920*, 63.4 (2020): 580-90.

Chirico, Paul, 'The Life of Rural Scenery', *Romanticism*, 26.2 (2020): 191-201.

Edwall, Christy, 'John Clare's Poetic Binomials', *Romanticism*, 26.2 (2020): 116-27.

Falke, Cassandra, 'Thinking With Birds: John Clare and the Phenomenology of Perception', *Romanticism*, 26.2 (2020): 180-90.

Francois, Anne-Lise, 'Passing Impasse', *Comparative Literature*, 72.2 (2020): 240-57.

Fulford, Tim, 'Ecopoetics and Boyopoetics: Bloomfield, Clare, and the Nature of Lyric', *European Romantic Review*, 31.5 (2020): 541-57.

Gorji, Mina, 'John Clare and the Language of Listening', *Romanticism*, 26.2 (2020): 153-67.

Heyes, Robert, '"My Unceasing Scribblings in Favour of John Clare": Lord Radstock's Letters to John Taylor', *JCSJ*, 39 (2020): 41-53.

Houghton-Walker, Sarah, 'Forms of Repetition in "The Robins Nest"', *Romanticism*, 26.2 (2020): 139-52.

Jackson-Houlston, C. M., '"Familiar Birds": John Clare, Vernacular Knowledge, and Poetic Precedents', *JCSJ*, 39 (2020): 71-84.

Jones, Clare, 'Bat, Bat, Come Under My Hat', *Keats-Shelley Review*, 33.1 (2019): 122-26.

Lafford, Erin, '"Mild health I see thee": Clare and Bloomfield at the Limits of Pastoral', *European Romantic Review*, 31.5 (2020): 527-40.

— 'John Clare, Herbalism, and Elegy', *Romanticism*, 26.2 (2020): 202-13.

Mackenney, Francesca, 'John Clare: Undersong', *Romanticism*, 26.2 (2020): 168-79.

McEathron, Scott, 'Nineteenth-Century Poetic Tributes and Elegies to Robert Bloomfield', *European Romantic Review*, 31.5 (2020): 637-52.

Nicholson, Michael, 'Unheard Swarms: John Clare and Romantic Entomology', *The Wordsworth Circle*, 51.3 (2020): 338-59.

Poetzsch, Markus, 'John Clare and the "Truth of Taste"', *JCSJ*, 39 (2020): 55-67.

Porter, Dahlia, 'Specimen Poetics: Botany, Reanimation, and the Romantic Collection', *Representations*, 139 (2017): 60-94.

Stout, Daniel, 'Open Field: On John Clare and the Crisis of our Critical Method', *The Wordsworth Circle*, 51.3 (2020): 377-95.

Suetta, Zachary, 'Blurred Boundaries: Anger, Identity and Satire in John Clare's Don Juan', *JCSJ*, 39 (2020): 85-100.

Tomaiuolo, Saverio, 'A Poet is Born, not Mad(e): John Clare's Afterlives', *Textus*, 2 (2020): 77-96.

Weiner, Stephanie Kuduk, 'At Home in the Working Countryside: Clare's Metaphysics of Agricultural Labour', *Romanticism*, 26.2 (2020): 128-38.

Wolfson, Susan J., 'Stories in Stones', *The Byron Journal*, 48.2 (2020): 101-17.

Other publications and projects

Haskins, Lola, *Asylum: Improvisations on John Clare* (Pittsburgh, PA.: University of Pittsburgh Press, 2019) (poetry collection).

Wojahn, David, 'Homage to John Clare', *Michigan Quarterly Review*, 59.1 (2020): 19-20 (poem).

'Wanderer in the Storm', Julius von Leypold (German, 1806–1874), 1835, oil on canvas. The Metropolitan Museum of Art, New York.

Reviews

Musical Settings of Clare: A Review Essay

Settings reviewed in this essay include:

North and Beyond. Divine Art Recordings Group. 2008. £6.99 – £9.50.

The Far Country – 26 English Songs. Divine Art Recordings group. 2007. £8.95 – £12.50.

Songs of Love and Loss. Presto Classical. 2007. £15.50.

Music of Judith Shatin and Peter Child. New World Records. 1991. £15.99.

At Midnight: Songs and Chamber Music. Signum Classics. 2010. £12.

The NMC Songbook (4 CDs). Chandos. 2015. £19.98.

Elektra Mourns. Presto Classical. 2017. £11.75.

The Little Toilings of the Honeybee. La Patsboom Productions. 2017. £9.99.

Eight Song Settings from the Poems of John Clare. Claudio Records. 2005. £6.00.

Clare's Journey. Claudio Records. 2012. £3.00.

Four Sonnets of John Clare. Julian Phillips. Edition Peters. 2002, rev.2015.

Love Songs for Mary Joyce. Julian Phillips. Edition Peters. 2016. £41.95.

In the first edition of the *John Clare Society Journal* (1982) Trevor Hold wrote an article about the many musical settings of the poet's work. That was nearly forty years ago and it is time that the work of composers since then was acknowledged. What follows is certainly not a comprehensive account of all the settings that have been written since 1980—I have not, for instance, ventured into the rich field of folk music—but I shall try to show something of the variety of ways in which composers have responded to Clare's words. Where possible I have given details of relevant CDs, but often individual tracks can be downloaded as MP3s, and many pieces can be heard on YouTube or Spotify.

The BBC programme in the Words and Music series on Radio 3 on 31 January 2016 was called 'The Village Minstrel' and comprised texts and music inspired by Clare. But the only setting of a poem by Clare himself was by John Jeffreys: 'Little Trotty Wagtail', a poem that holds the record for the highest number of musical settings! Jeffreys, who died in 2010, was a sensitive composer of English song, in the tradition of Ivor Gurney, Gerald Finzi and Peter Warlock, and this is a charming setting for tenor and piano. It is included in two different collections of Jeffreys's songs, with Ian Partridge accompanied by Jennifer Partridge on a CD called *Northumberland and Beyond* (2008), and James Gilchrist accompanied by Anna Tilbrook on a CD called *The Far Country: 26 English Songs* (2007). Working in a slightly more modern idiom, Geoffrey Kimpton's song cycle, *Six Love Songs of John Clare* (2007), is for baritone and piano, and can be found on a CD titled *Songs of Love and Loss* sung by Mark Rawlinson accompanied by Peter Lawson.

Voice and piano is the customary pairing, but I have listened to several Clare settings where the voice has a different and sometimes rather unusual accompaniment. For instance, Stephen Dodgson (mentioned in Hold's article) wrote his *Four Poems of John Clare* (1963) for voice and guitar, a combination that is reminiscent of Elizabethan songs for voice and lute. Dodgson's songs can be heard on YouTube in two different versions, one for soprano, the other for tenor (and yes, one song is 'Little Trotty Wagtail'). Peter Child, in a very different musical style, wrote for a less intimate ensemble in his *Clare Cycle: four settings from the poetry of John Clare* (1985). This cycle, which, interestingly, includes 'The Yellowhammer's Nest', as well as the more frequently set 'I Am', is for high soprano with flute/alto flute, oboe, clarinet/bass clarinet, two violins, viola, cello, double bass, percussion, and piano. Child is Professor of Music at the Massachusetts Institute of Technology, and clearly delights in experimental composition. The instruments in this song cycle provide a variety of timbres which he exploits in a very exciting way; they are not simply an accompaniment but have an interest of their own. The vocal part, too, impressively sung by Joan Heller on the CD *Shatin and Child*, demands a variety of vocal techniques. In 'The Yellowhammer's Nest', not an obvious choice for musical setting, the vocal part is spoken, with the instruments providing illustrative sounds as suggested by the text. Here, then, the words are perfectly audible, but that is not quite the case for all the songs.

Stephen Burgon (d. 2010) is best known for his television theme music (for instance *Brideshead Revisited*), but he also wrote a lot of church music, and set seven songs to poems written by Clare while he was in Northampton Asylum: *A Vision* (1991) for tenor with string orchestra. Ian Venables, too, uses strings to accompany the singer in a cycle of four songs for tenor with string quartet: *Invite, to Eternity* (1997). His lovely lyrical songs, like Jeffreys's, are in the style of English art song. They are beautifully sung by Andrew Kennedy with the Dante Quartet on the CD *At Midnight: Songs and Chamber Music of Ian Venables*. A different instrument was chosen by Terence Greaves (1933-2009): his *Rustic Poems of John Clare* (the third one being another 'Little Trotty Wagtail') is for high voice and clarinet. I have not been able to find a performance on CD, but I did find a video of the songs on YouTube made by Joann Martinson Davis and Trevor Davis (academics at the Louisiana Tech University School of Music) at home during lockdown in 2020.

A rather more unusual and fascinating setting was written by Anthony Gilbert. He set 'Those Fenny Bells' for treble, counter-tenor and, appropriately, tubular bells. This song (though with a mezzo-soprano instead of a boy treble) can be heard on one of the four CDs that constitute the *NMC Songbook: 20th Anniversary* (2009). Another CD from the *NMC Songbook* has a Clare song by Brian Elias, 'Meet me in the Green Glen'. He later set another four poems to make up a cycle of five songs that is part of the CD *Elektra Mourns* (2017). These haunting songs are for unaccompanied singer and are sung by both Roderick Williams (baritone) and Susan Bickley (mezzo-soprano) as the accomplished soloists.

With *The little toilings of the Honeybee*, a CD by La Pat, we enter a different song world. La Pat, or Patty Trossèl to give her full name, is classically trained, but composes and performs in a more popular idiom. This CD consists of nine settings of poems by Clare, plus two of John Dowland's songs. La Pat is the lead singer and also plays piano, accordion and keyboards. There are three other female singers on the disc, who provide backing vocals and play cello and violin. The only CDs that I know of that are devoted *entirely* to Clare are those based on Terence Deadman's work, which are sold by the Society. *Eight Song Settings* combines songs with spoken verse. The other, *Clare's Journey*, is the narrative of Clare's journey home from the Epping asylum, combining song and spoken dialogue, and was reviewed by Janet Ingamells in the JCS *Newsletter* No.119 (October 2013).

The majority of Clare settings are for solo voice. However, in 2014, to commemorate the 150th anniversary of Clare's death, Somtow Sucharitkul was commissioned by The Fairhaven Singers, and set 'Graves of infants' and 'Insects' for chamber choir. These graphic pieces were included in a concert in Peterborough on 17 May 2014 (reviewed by me in *Newsletter* No. 122, October 2014). On a rather larger scale, Julian Philips's *Song's Eternity* (2002) is a work for choir and organ that was commissioned by the Musicians' Benevolent Fund for the combined choirs of Westminster Abbey, Westminster Cathedral and St Paul's Cathedral.

Philips, a professor at the Guildhall School of Music & Drama, has composed many works on a large scale, but he has also turned to British and American poets for the intimacy of song cycles for solo voice and piano. Two of these cycles are settings of Clare, which were commissioned by the Wigmore Hall. *Four Sonnets of John Clare* is for baritone and piano and was performed at the Wigmore Hall in 2002 by Sir Thomas Allen and Graham Johnson. *Love Songs for Mary Joyce* takes Clare's journey out of Essex as its narrative frame, setting six Mary poems. Unlike Deadman's *Clare's Journey*, there is no spoken narrative; rather, we follow Clare on an emotional journey. Philips draws on the traditions of both folk and art song, composing a vocal lines that allow the words to be clearly heard. The piano accompaniment is as interesting as the vocal part, adding both atmosphere and another layer of meaning to the songs. In the first song, for instance, the piano seems to indicate Clare's agitated state of mind. In the third song, 'To Mary: I sleep with thee, and wake with thee', the three stanzas of the poem are separated by short prose extracts from *Recollections of Journey from Essex* which tell about Clare's dream of Mary one night on the road. They are sung in a sort of melodic recitative, picking up on the theme of the poem and adding the poignancy of autobiography. The cycle was performed at the Wigmore Hall by James Gilchirst and Anna Tilbrook in 2016. The sheet music for these two song cycles is published by Edition Peters, but they are not on CD.

Philips is currently working on a set of nine creative transcriptions of some of the folk melodies Clare transcribed in his fiddle books, which he tells me he has '"arranged", or maybe recomposed... for clarinet and violin'. This work forms part of Simon Kövesi's *The Meeting* project and is being recorded.

Valerie Pedlar

Working Verse in Victorian Scotland.
By KIRSTIE BLAIR. Oxford University
Press. 2019. Pp. 235. £65.

Kirstie Blair's book is the most
important I have seen in the
developing study of labouring-class
poets and verse culture, for several
reasons. It revives and analyses an
area of Scottish culture that was
richly celebrated in its time but fell
into neglect and disparagement. It
deals brilliantly with what one might
call the sociology of poetry. And it
grasps the nettle of a problem which
much work on labouring-class poetry
(including my own) has fumbled or
ignored: the all-important question
of value. Professor Blair brings fresh
ideas, particularly from post-colonial
sources, to this topic, arguing radically
that labouring-class poetry, her
'working verse' in Victorian Scotland,
did not aspire to Romantic ideals of
originality and high aesthetic value
that have become a general standard, or
as something that would 'reward close
readers with ever-new insights into
the interaction of language and form'
(p. 2) as we might read a canonical
poet such as Keats or Milton. Rather,
they aspired to contribute in a widely
understood, conventional (purposely
following a set of conventions) way,
to traditions that were often local
or regional, often musical—a most
important point, since so many verses
were *both* poems and songs—and were,
above all, social: again in contrast to
the familiar idea of the Romantic
'lonely poet surrounded by nature'
(John Sitter's phrase). The question of
what purpose poetry serves can more
readily be answered under this model:
it serves a culture, much fragmented
by the Scottish diaspora, drawing it
together around popular and accessible
outlets, the poetry columns in the
newspapers, pamphlet and broadside
publication, reciting or singing, and
performative presentations. Printed
volumes of poetry, again often taken
as the gold standard of value in poetry,
are far less central in this model, and
indeed might sometimes represent a
diluted and over-respectable bottled
version of their original social and
verbal energies.

This is a poetry that writes
of common experience, examines
changes in society and working
practices, celebrates the land and its
beauty, and shares other areas ranging
from nursery and family verse, to
working verse, to the pleasures of
humorous and ostensibly 'bad' poetry.
It offers social and political analysis,
and sometimes protest as well as
celebration of common, local, and
national cultures.

Part of the backlash against
popular nineteenth-century Scottish
poetry was a reaction against
widespread claims that Scotland was
the 'Peasant Poet Queen of the Nation'
with (as the poet Henry Shanks called
it), a bard in every village. The obvious
critical response to this common idea
of Scots poetry is that it represented
quantity over quality. But after setting
out her stall firmly and clearly in the
Introduction, Blair begins to unpick
this binary in an opening chapter on
'The World of Work'. What was the
'work of poetry', for all these many
village and town verse-makers? What
were the village poets doing? She
significantly notes that there were
also very many such poets throughout
the Anglophone world, and that it
was not just a Scottish phenomenon.
Nevertheless she sees the idea of
Scottish labouring-class poetic
supremacy as useful in one way at

least, in that it makes it a 'valuable test case for the ways in which local and provincial working-class verse cultures were valued and utilized for social, cultural, and political ends' (p. 21). For an individual, verse could be seen as a noteworthy step in self-education, even for those who had other plans, a 'signal of self-improvement, intelligence and industry' (p. 176), that would be valued. But to write verse leads directly into the social aspect of things, epitomised here by a section of this chapter headed 'Shaping Communities: Newspaper Poetry and the Construction of the Local Poet'. A volume of poetry may be a private space for an individual poet that we then read, but the 'Poet's Corner' of the local newspaper or the popular periodical is a social space, a free-for-all and, importantly, a dialogue. Poems respond to other poems, and there is always a penumbra of correspondence and editorial comment, and a competition for space and for perceived quality. In a publication as focused as the Dundee's *People's Journal* (the subject of an important recent anthology by Blair that feeds into the present work[1]), which called itself 'A Penny Saturday paper devoted to the interests of the Working Classes', this social and interactive aspect of poetry becomes intense: there are formal competitions, spin-off anthologies, poets rise and fall, interact and compete. Blair looks at individuals like Ellen Johnston, who identified herself as 'The Factory Girl', and the flow of epistolary poems between her and other correspondents in Glasgow's *Penny Post* (pp. 56-7). Some poets indeed 'spun off' into

their own dedicated volumes, often supported or printed by the newspapers themselves, and perhaps utilising the subscription model to draw on the social capital they have built up in their local work.

It is difficult even to summarise adequately the huge amount of important work that is done in this volume. The four chapters that follow and complete it look at nursery and family verse and the culture of *Whistle-Binkie*, at how verse perceives and understands Scotland, Industry and the world of work, and, in the final chapter, at Humour, Satire, and the rise of the Bad Poet. There is a great deal to be said about all four topics, but for this reviewer the most interesting is the last one, particularly its refusal to handle that dangerous phrase 'bad poet' with the careful tongs of 'scare quotes', as many of us would reflexly do. The question of value and self-perception in Scottish poetry emerges in the over-familiar name of McGonagall, among others, and is dealt with in balanced, thoughtful, and welcome ways here.

This is a much needed book, both for the history of poetry and for the questions of value that invariably follows the recovery of neglected texts.

John Goodridge
Nottingham Trent University

---

1   *Poets of the People's Journal* (Glasgow: ASLS, 2016)

The Poetry of Clare, Hopkins, Thomas, and Gurney: Lyric Individualism.
By ANDREW HODGSON. London: Palgrave Macmillan. 2019. Pp. xviii + 336. £51.99.

In this thoughtful study, Andrew Hodgson examines poems that seem to crack, even to break down, under the pressure of their authors' individuality. The 'lyric individualism' of his subtitle names the poetic mode in which an author's individuality exacts accommodations in form and language. Lyric expressivity looks different here.

Hodgson traces a line of four English poets writing from the early nineteenth century to the early twentieth: John Clare, Gerard Manley Hopkins, Edward Thomas, and Ivor Gurney. According to Hodgson, these writers describe their experiences of selfhood in ways that derive meaning from their singularity rather than from their universality. Similarly, these poets' depictions of the world outside the self tend in Hodgson's view to prioritize the particularity of their ways of observing and interpreting it. Hodgson takes seriously these aspects of their subject matter. He aspires to keep clearly in view, and to honour, the unconventional strangeness of their representations of self and world.

Throughout, Hodgson is interested in how these poets make their individuality register in language. He seeks out poems in which the author's 'personality is a matter of voice, of idiom and movement' (p. 7). In reading such poems, Hodgson homes in on distortions and contortions of syntax. He presses hard on moments of obscurity, inarticulacy, and incoherence when semantic meaning refuses to resolve itself into any one paraphrasable idea. These moments convey for Hodgson 'a more-than-ordinarily intense sense of language's recalcitrance' and inadequacy (p. 241). It is for this reason that they test the scope and limits of lyric as a verbal art.

One way Hodgson isolates lyric individualism is to measure these writers' language against the norms of their literary environments. All four of his poets are to be found on the margins of the intellectual and artistic mainstream of their day, and all four came to a full critical appreciation only posthumously. These facts suggest for Hodgson that violating aesthetic and linguistic norms was an enduring strategy for asserting a stubborn uniqueness. At the same time, though, all four writers recognized that language is a shared resource, a collective technology. They wanted to make it serve their purposes and express their ideas, feelings, and experiences rather than to invent a wholly personal, self-contained idiom. At the end of the day, they wrote poems, and their craftsmanship often entailed testing the scope and limits of English as a language and of poetry as a medium. According to Hodgson, each writer's voice is the product of this negotiation—between resistance and conformity, expressivity and communication, feeling and word, self and syntax.

Two other, related negotiations are central to Hodgson's account. The first is between self-knowledge and self-discovery, the second between solitude and connection. According to Hodgson, Clare, Hopkins, Thomas, and Gurney all 'trace the contours of the self as it exists in a given instant or under a given impulse, seeking truthfulness to voice and feeling as they occur in the moment' (p. 33). In Thomas's poems, as Hodgson explains, 'A truly personal voice... manifests rather than asserts individual character... depicting "self-expression" less as a translation of a pre-existing identity into language than as an effort to uncover and impress one's innermost nature upon it in the process of composition' (p. 170, p. 171). For Gurney, this happens by means of a language that conveys a sense of urgency and spontaneity as well as eccentricity. Hopkins, similarly, strives to convey inspiration, ease, and the natural cadences of the speaking voice, especially in moments of strong feeling. 'Repeatedly, emotion in Hopkins's poetry seems unpremeditated', Hodgson writes (p. 130). Often in Clare's verse, too, 'a unique intensity of feeling or vision threatens to overwhelm his powers of eloquence or break through standard forms of expression' (p. 52). Hodgson locates such moments in poems written throughout Clare's career. His 'irrepressibly off-kilter idiom' collides with a printed standard, invigorates highly conventional modes such as the song, and manages to keep alive many layers of potential meaning by resisting the ordering and subordinating powers of punctuation (p. 65).

The dialectic between a sense of solitary isolation on the one hand and a desire for human connection on the other is in my view the most poignant strand in Hodgson's story. All these poets give words to feelings of intense loneliness and to an often painful sense that marching to their own drummers cast them forever at a distance from the other members of the band. They often despaired of finding an appreciative audience, and this despair seems to have nurtured their eccentricity. Yet their poems also find myriad ways to reach toward communion. Gurney keeps common experience and the sufferings of others in view. Hopkins's desire for intimacy with his readers prompts attempts to manage the off-putting strangeness of his language as well as experiments in hailing readers and drawing them into a circle of 'human contact' and 'Christ's loving solicitude' (p. 165, p. 149). Thomas writes poems of love and friendship, and crafts an autobiographical poetics whose reticence in balanced by its candor. Clare seems to speak from his heart directly to that of his readers, trusting them—that is, us—to conjure him and feel with him.

Hodgson is a generous and scrupulous reader. He engages in a sustained conversation with these four poets as well as with the rich critical heritage and poetic afterlives their work has inspired. A short epilogue considers the writing of Charlotte Mew, Stephen Spender, and Elizabeth Jennings.

Stephanie Kuduk Weiner
Wesleyan University

Contributors

SIR JONATHAN BATE is Clare's biographer and the editor of the Faber and Faber edition of his *Selected Poems*.

ALEX BROADHEAD is Lecturer in English Language and Literature at the University of Liverpool, and his interests lie in the area of dialect in eighteenth and nineteenth-century literature. Linguistic creativity is a recurring focus of his work, which employs the tools of stylistics and sociolinguistics to illustrate how, for many of the writers of this period, dialect was a source of joyful experimentation. He has published on Wordsworth, Josiah Relph and (with Jane Hodson) Romantic-era fiction. His monograph, *The Language of Robert Burns: Style, Ideology and Identity*, came out in 2014. He has another in preparation, on the language of early dialect literature.

JOHN GOODRIDGE is Emeritus Professor of English at Nottingham Trent University, a Vice-President of the John Clare Society, and former editor of this journal. His publications include *John Clare and Community* (2012) and, with R.K.R. Thornton, *John Clare the Trespasser* (2016). He has edited critical material on Clare, editions of Bloomfield, John Dyer and labouring-class poets and, with Bridget Keegan, *A History of British Working-Class Literature* (2017). He continues to develop his Catalogue of Labouring-Class Poets.

ROBERT HAMBERGER has been shortlisted and highly commended for Forward prizes, appearing in the Forward Book of Poetry 2020. He has been awarded a Hawthornden Fellowship; his poetry has been featured as the Guardian Poem of the Week and in British, American, Irish and Japanese anthologies. He has published six poetry pamphlets and four full-length collections. *Blue Wallpaper* (published by Waterloo Press) was shortlisted for the 2020 Polari Prize. His prose memoir with poems *A Length of Road: finding myself in the footsteps of John Clare* was published by John Murray in June 2021. His website is www.roberthamberger.co.uk

BRIDGET KEEGAN is a Professor of English and Dean of Arts and Sciences at Creighton University in Omaha, Nebraska. She has published extensively on eighteenth-century and Romantic-period poetry. Her books include a volume of *Eighteenth-Century English Labouring-Class Poets* (2003), *British Labouring-class Nature Poetry, 1730–1837* (2008), and *The Eighteenth-Century Literature Handbook* (2009). Most recently she is the co-editor, with John Goodridge, of Cambridge University Press's *A History of British Working-Class Literature* (2017).

ERIN LAFFORD is currently a Postdoctoral Research Fellow in English at the University of Derby. She is completing her first book, *John Clare and the Poetry of Illness*, and has recently published essays on John Clare, Robert Bloomfield, and William Gilpin that explore these writers' explorations of illness, emotion, environment, and aesthetics. She is also co-editor of *Palgrave Advances in John Clare Studies* (Palgrave 2020), and book reviews editor of this journal. From October 2021 Erin will be a Departmental Lecturer in English Literature at the University of Oxford.

EMMA MASON is Professor and Head of English and Comparative Literary Studies at the University of Warwick. She has published widely on religion and poetry. Her last book was *Christina Rossetti: Poetry, Ecology, Faith* (Oxford University Press, 2018). With Mark Knight, she is series editor of Bloomsbury's monograph series, New Directions in Religion and Literature.

SCOTT McEATHRON is Professor of English at Southern Illinois University, Carbondale. He has written extensively on the relationship between labouring-class poetry and canonical Romanticism. In tandem with Simon Kövesi, he served as editor of *New Essays on John Clare: Poetry, Culture and Community* (Cambridge University Press, 2015). He has a continuing interest in Romantic-era painters and paintings with links to Lamb, Hazlitt, and Keats, and is developing new work on the publishing career of Edward Moxon, the poetic theory of Thomas Hardy, and early British detective fiction.

JAMES C. McKUSICK is Professor of English at the University of Missouri–Kansas City. He completed his B.A. at Dartmouth College and his Ph.D. at Yale University. He is the author of *Green Writing: Romanticism and Ecology* (2000) and *Coleridge's Philosophy of Language* (1986). He is co-editor of *Faustus: From the German of Goethe, translated by Samuel Taylor Coleridge* (2007) and *Literature and Nature: Four Centuries of Nature Writing* (2001). He serves as President of the Wordsworth-Coleridge Association and Executive Director of the John Clare Society of North America.

VALERIE PEDLAR is Chair of the John Clare Society. She retired from The Open University in 2004 after many years in adult education. Her specialist area was madness in Victorian fiction, culminating in her book, *The Most Dreadful Visitation: male madness in Victorian fiction*, and it was a fascination with theories and treatments of madness that led to her interest in Clare's life and work. Music, and especially singing, has always been an important part of her life; she has sung in a number of choirs ever since school days.

JENS PETERS is a dramaturg and independent researcher. After eight years in Great Britain between 2003 and 2012, he returned to Germany to pursue his twin passions, working in theatres in Berlin, Karlsruhe and most recently in Osnabrück, and lecturing at universities in Berlin, Munich, Karlsruhe, Osnabrück and Münster. His most recent work, a paper on birds in the poetry of John Clare and the German poet (and Clare translator) Esther Kinsky, is to be published at the end of 2021.

STEPHEN RIDGWELL completed a PhD in history at Sussex University in 2017 on representations of the English poacher *c.* 1831-1920. His work has since appeared in various journals and magazines including *Early Popular Visual Culture*, the *Journal of Victorian Culture*, *Rural History* and *History Today*. He is currently working on George Crabbe and pursuing a wider Romantic-period interest in the poacher.

FIONA STAFFORD is Professor of English at the University of Oxford and Fellow of the British Academy. In addition to her work on Romantic literature and Scottish and Irish literature, she writes about the natural world. Recent books include *The Brief Life of Flowers* (2018), *The Long, Long Life of Trees* (2016), and *Local Attachments* (2010). She is a regular contributor to Radio, recently appearing on *In Our Time* (Robert Burns), *Natural Histories*, *The Essay*, and *Keats Walks North*, a walk-and-talk documentary about Keats's Scottish tour.

NIC WILSON is a writer living in the chalklands of Hertfordshire. After an MA in English Literature (focusing on the interplay between science and narrative in the works of Ford Madox Ford) and twelve years teaching English A Level, she now combines her love of the written word and the natural world as a *Guardian* Country Diarist. Most recently Nic was a contributor to the collection *Women on Nature* (Unbound, 2021), edited by Katharine Norbury. She continues to research the lives of Clare's contemporaries – including her own ancestors – and is currently working on a memoir exploring our engagement with everyday landscapes.

SARAH ZIMMERMAN is Professor of English at Fordham University. She has written on John Clare in *Romanticism, Lyricism, and History* (SUNY Press, 1999) and in essays on his birds-nesting poems, his literary career, and the history of his critical reception. She has also focused on the history of private life and on the early history of public lectures on poetry. Her recent work includes *The Romantic Literary Lecture in Britain* (Oxford University Press, 2019).

Abbreviations

BIOGRAPHY *John Clare, A Biography*, Jonathan Bate (London: Picador, 2003)

BY HIMSELF *John Clare By Himself*, ed. Eric Robinson and David Powell (Ashington and Manchester: Mid-NAG and Carcanet, 1996)

COTTAGE TALES *John Clare, Cottage Tales*, ed. Eric Robinson, David Powell and P.M.S. Dawson (Ashington and Manchester: Mid-NAG and Carcanet, 1993)

CRITICAL HERITAGE *Clare: The Critical Heritage*, ed. Mark Storey (London: Routledge & Kegan Paul, 1973)

EARLY POEMS (I–II) *The Early Poems of John Clare*, ed. Eric Robinson, David Powell and Margaret Grainger (Oxford: Clarendon Press, 1989)

JOHN CLARE IN CONTEXT, ed. Hugh Haughton, Adam Phillips and Geoffrey Summerfield (Cambridge: Cambridge University Press, 1994)

JCSJ *The John Clare Society Journal* (1982–)

LATER POEMS *The Later Poems of John Clare*, ed. Eric Robinson, David Powell and Margaret Grainger (Oxford: Clarendon Press, 1984)

LETTERS *The Letters of John Clare*, ed. Mark Storey (Oxford: Clarendon Press, 1985)

MIDDLE PERIOD (I–II) *John Clare, Poems of the Middle Period 1822–1837*, ed. Eric Robinson, David Powell and P.M.S. Dawson (Oxford: Clarendon Press, 1996); (III–IV) (1998); (V) (2003)

MIDSUMMER CUSHION *John Clare, The Midsummer Cushion*, ed. Kelsey Thornton and Anne Tibble (Ashington and Manchester: Mid-NAG and Carcanet, revised edition, 1990)

NATURAL HISTORY *The Natural History Prose Writings of John Clare*, ed. Margaret Grainger (Oxford: Clarendon Press, 1983)

NEW APPROACHES *John Clare, New Approaches*, ed. John Goodridge and Simon Kövesi (Helpston: John Clare Society, 2000)

NORTHBOROUGH SONNETS *John Clare, Northborough Sonnets*, ed. Eric Robinson, David Powell and P.M.S. Dawson (Ashington and Manchester: Mid-NAG and Carcanet, 1995)

PROSE *The Prose of John Clare*, ed. J.W. and Anne Tibble (London: Routledge & Kegan Paul, 1951, reprinted 1970)

SHEPHERD'S CALENDAR *John Clare, The Shepherd's Calendar*, ed. Eric Robinson, Geoffrey Summerfield and David Powell (Oxford: Oxford University Press, revised edition, 1993)